GYMNASTICS FOR KIDS

The Ultimate Beginner's Guide: A Complete Resource
for Parents and Children to Start Their Gymnastics
Journey at Home

JOSIE QUAID

Contents

Introduction

As you sit there, watching your child gleefully flip and tumble across the living room floor, a thought crosses your mind: "How can I channel this boundless energy into something structured like gymnastics, without immediate access to a local gym or formal training?" It's a common scenario many parents face— eager to support their child's interest in gymnastics but unsure where to start. This is where I step in, armed with a mission to make gymnastics accessible to all children, no matter their location or the depth of their pockets.

This book was born from my deep-rooted passion for helping children become more active, and to have access to all the most enriching activities. My experience and dedication to promoting safety, embracing diversity, and the sheer joy of learning new physical skills have driven me to create this guide. This isn't just a book; it's a movement toward building a foundational platform for young enthusiasts across diverse backgrounds.

This guide is designed to be your ally in fostering your child's gymnastics skills from the comfort of your home. Aimed primarily at elementary school-aged children, it compiles essential safety guidelines, simple foundational exercises, and motivating stories from real gymnasts who have navigated their paths through the ups and downs of this sport. It's structured to be followed easily, ensuring that any parent, regardless of their prior knowledge of gymnastics, can become a supportive coach cheering from the sidelines.

Understanding the pivotal role of physical activity in child development, I've included research-backed insights showing how gymnastics can significantly enhance fitness, coordination, discipline, and self-esteem. For instance, studies indicate that children engaged in regular physical activity score better physically and exhibit enhanced cognitive functioning and emotional resilience. My own experiences sparked my journey into writing this book—watching my children transform as they find confidence and joy in their newfound physical capabilities.

In this book, you'll find each chapter thoughtfully crafted to guide you and your child through the initial steps of gymnastics. From setting up a safe practice environment at home to advancing through basic techniques and celebrating each small victory, every page is designed to be engaging and informative.

As we turn this page together, remember that embarking on this gymnastic journey is about more than just physical health—it's about bonding as a family, embracing challenges, and having a tremendous amount of fun along the way. Whether your living room turns into a makeshift gym or you dedicate a special corner for practice, the moments you create while supporting your child's gymnastic endeavors will be invaluable.

Let's jump into this adventure together and start instilling resilience, strength, and joy in your child, one somersault at a time.

ONE

Getting Started with Gymnastics at Home

D o you remember the exhilaration of building forts as a child? Just as you creatively transformed living rooms into castles or caves without a blueprint, starting gymnastics at home with your kids can be similarly inventive and exciting.

However, unlike the haphazard joy of fort-building, setting up a home gymnastics practice requires careful consideration to ensure safety and effectiveness. This chapter will guide you through selecting the perfect spot in your home, preparing the area to accommodate gymnastics activities, and making sure the environment is safe and conducive to your child's gymnastic adventures.

1.1 Choosing the Right Space at Home for Gymnastics

When it comes to gymnastics, not just any space will do. The joy and safety of your child's gymnastics practice hinge significantly on where they practice.

First, let's talk about the **space requirements**. Ideally, you'll need a clear, obstruction-free area where your child can tumble, jump, and stretch without risk. A space of at least 10x10 feet is a good starting point, but you may need more room for activities like running or swinging. Ensure the area you choose is away from furniture, sharp corners, or hard surfaces that could pose a risk during activities.

Next, the **surface considerations** are crucial. Gymnastics involves a lot of impact on the body, and practicing on a hard or uneven surface can lead to injuries. This is why investing in a high-quality gymnastics mat is must. Look for mats that are at least two inches thick to provide adequate cushioning for falls and jumps. Foam tiles or interlocking mats can also be a good alternative, especially if you need a temporary setup that you can put away after practice. These surfaces help in absorbing impact and provide a non-slip texture to keep those little feet stable.

Another pivotal aspect is the **environmental safety** of your chosen area. Double-check that there are no overhead obstacles like ceiling fans or low-hanging light fixtures that could interfere with jumping or lifting movements. Also, be sure there's no furniture that could tip over if your child were to accidentally push against it with force. All furniture in your house should be secured properly to the walls to prevent tipping.

Adequate lighting is important, too, not just for visibility but also to ensure that your child can accurately judge distances and execute movements safely. Natural light is best, but if that's not available, make sure the area is well-lit with overhead lights that evenly illuminate the space.

Additionally, good ventilation is important, especially as gymnastics can be a high-intensity workout leading to quick heat build-up. It's best if nearby windows can be opened or a fan is available to keep the air fresh.

Lastly, **adjustability for different exercises** should be considered. Gymnastics is not a one-size-fits-all sport, and as your child progresses, they'll likely venture into different types of activities that require different amounts of space and equipment. The area should be versatile enough to adapt to these needs.

For example, if your child moves from floor exercises to apparatus work, you might need to reorganize the space to accommodate a junior balance beam safely. The key is to have a space that can evolve with your child's gymnastic proficiency and interest.

Reflection Section

Take a moment to reflect on the space you're considering for gymnastics at home. Visualize your child practicing in this area and ask yourself:

- Is it spacious and free from hazards?
- Is the surface suitable and safe for all types of movements?
- Does the lighting and ventilation set the stage for a good practice environment?
- Can the space be adjusted for different activities as your child grows and explores more gymnastics disciplines?

This reflection can help solidify your decision and ensure that the space you set up contributes positively to your child's gymnastics experience, keeping them safe and excited about their practice. Remember, the right environment can make all the difference in cultivating a love for gymnastics in your child and turning your home into a foundation for their gymnastic development.

1.2 Essential Gymnastics Equipment for Beginners

When you begin your home gymnastics setup, the right equipment enhances the learning experience and ensures safety. Let's walk through some of the foundational pieces you'll need to get started.

First and foremost, as mentioned before, every budding gymnast needs a high-quality gymnastics mat. Mats are the cornerstone of safe gymnastics practice at home as they cushion the landing for various activities and help prevent injuries. But not all mats are created equal, and choosing the right one is crucial.

For most home environments, panel mats are highly versatile. They fold easily for storage, offer sufficient padding, and can be linked with additional mats to expand the practice area. These typically come in thicknesses ranging from 1.5 to 2.5 inches, providing a balance between cushioning and stability. For younger children or activities that require more cushioning, thicker mats or crash pads can be appropriate.

Another piece of equipment to consider is the balance beam. Low beams that sit directly on the floor are perfect for beginners and reduce the risk of serious falls. They allow young gymnasts to practice skills safely, building confidence and balance. Foam beams or sectional beams covered with synthetic suede give a feel similar to competition beams without the height risk, making them ideal for home use. As your child progresses, a low wooden beam might be the next addition, offering more of a professional feel.

Horizontal bars for home use come in various designs, but adjustable single bars are advisable when starting. These can be set to a lower height as your child learns and later raised as they gain more skill and confidence. Make sure whatever model you choose has a sturdy base and provides good grip and stability.

When it comes to cost-effective solutions, remember that quality shouldn't be compromised for price, especially when safety is involved. However, there are ways to be economical without risking your child's safety. Shopping during sales, purchasing second-hand equipment from reliable sources, or even DIY solutions for simpler apparatus like balance beams can reduce costs. For instance, a DIY beam can be made using a wooden plank covered with a foam layer and a non-slip surface, all of which can be sourced relatively inexpensively and assembled with basic DIY skills.

Storage is another important aspect to consider, especially if you have limited space. Most gymnastics mats can be folded or rolled up when not in use. Wall-mounted racks can be another great option for hanging mats, keeping them off the floor and reducing clutter. For beams and bars, look for models that can be easily disassembled or have a small footprint. Ensuring your equipment is stored correctly will not only keep your home tidy but also prolong the life of the equipment by protecting it from damage.

Each piece of equipment should be chosen carefully, considering both the gymnast's current skill level and potential progression. This forward-thinking approach ensures that you invest in equipment that grows with your child's abilities, offering the best value for your money and the longest span of use. These tips will help you create a safe, functional, and enjoyable gymnastics practice area right at home, enabling your child to explore and excel in gymnastics with confidence and joy.

1.3 Understanding Gymnastics Terms: A Glossary for Kids and Parents

You're getting closer to helping your child start their gymnastics practice at home. As you guide them through their paces, knowing the correct terms not only helps in executing movements correctly but also boosts your child's confidence as they feel more connected to the sport. This glossary is here to demystify the jargon, making gymnastics lingo accessible and fun for both of you. Let's break down some key terms that you'll come across frequently as you explore the wonderful world of gymnastics together.

Aerial: A gymnastic skill where the gymnast performs a cartwheel or walkover without using their hands. This advanced skill requires strength, balance, and precise technique.

Arabesque: A ballet-inspired position where one leg is extended straight behind the body, and the other leg supports the gymnast's weight, often performed on the beam or floor to demonstrate grace and flexibility.

Back Walkover: A skill where the gymnast begins in a standing position, arches backward into a bridge position, and then lifts one leg to walk over into a standing position again.

Beam: A narrow, slightly elevated horizontal bar used in gymnastics routines. Gymnasts perform a variety of skills and dance elements on the beam, showcasing their balance, strength, and agility.

Cartwheel: One of the foundational skills every young gymnast learns. A cartwheel is a sideways rotary movement of the body. The gymnast starts standing, places their hands on the floor, and kicks their legs over in a wheel-like motion, finishing by standing again. It looks like the spokes of a wheel turning over. In a routine, you might see a gymnast perform a cartwheel followed by a backbend.

Dismount: The skill or movement used by a gymnast to leave an apparatus, such as the bars, beam, or rings. It often involves a jump, flip, or twist and is critical for a clean finish.

Handspring: This term refers to a springing movement executed by the hands. In a handspring, the gymnast's body flips forward or backward, with hands touching the ground to push off and propel the body over. It's thrilling to watch and fun to do, and it builds from a solid foundation in basic gymnastics skills.

Handstand: A skill where the gymnast balances on their hands with their body extended vertically. Handstands are foundational to many other skills and are practiced to develop strength and control.

Pike: A position where the body is bent at the hips, with legs straight and together, forming a sort of 'V' shape with the body. This position is crucial for various jumps and leaps, helping gymnasts achieve a crisp, clean line that judges look for in competitions.

Round-off: A gymnastics move similar to a cartwheel but with a twist at the end. The gymnast starts with a running approach, turns in mid-air, and lands on both feet together, often used to gain momentum for further skills.

Routine: A sequence of skills and movements performed by a gymnast on an apparatus or on the floor. Routines are choreographed to demonstrate a gymnast's abilities and are judged in competitions.

Somersault: A forward or backward roll where the gymnast's body rotates completely around an imaginary horizontal axis, head over heels. A somersault is usually performed on the floor.

Split: A position where the legs are extended in opposite directions, either forward-backward (front split) or side-to-side (side split), with the aim of having both legs and hips in a straight line.

Spotting: The act of assisting a gymnast during the execution of a skill to ensure safety and correct technique. A spotter provides support and guidance, especially during the learning stages.

Straddle: A position where the legs are spread wide apart to the sides, forming a 'V' shape with the body. The straddle position is used in various skills and jumps to demonstrate flexibility.

Tuck: In a tuck position, the knees are brought close to the chest, and the body is curled into a compact ball-like form. This position is essential for performing various rolls and flips, where tight body formation helps in rotating efficiently. You might see this term come to life when a gymnast performs a back tuck, where they jump backward into a somersault, knees pulled tightly to the chest.

Tumbling: A series of acrobatic skills performed in sequence on the floor, including flips, handsprings, and twists. Tumbling passes are a highlight in floor routines.

To assist in the learning process, especially for visual learners, each of these terms in your printed guide is accompanied by simple illustrations that depict the position or movement. These visual aids ensure that both you and your child can quickly grasp what each term represents, making your practice sessions more effective and enjoyable.

Remember, this glossary isn't just a list of terms; it's the beginning of a language that you and your child will use to communicate in the exciting realm of gymnastics. Each term learned is a step further in understanding and loving the sport. As you progress, these words will become a natural part of your conversation about gymnastics, bringing clarity and precision to your discussions and practice.

Whether you're watching a gymnastics competition on TV or coaching your child through their routines at home, these terms will enhance your appreciation and enjoyment of the sport, making every flip, roll, and jump an exciting and understood element of gymnastics.

1.4 Basic Warm-Up Exercises for Safe Practice

Before a painter begins a masterpiece, they sketch outlines; similarly, every gymnast should start with a good warm-up, no matter their age or skill level. It's the blueprint for a successful practice session. Warming up is essential not just as a ritual but as a proactive measure to safeguard against injuries and to prime the body and mind for the demands of gymnastics.

Engaging in a series of dynamic movements prepares the muscles, enhances flexibility, and boosts cardiovascular readiness, getting the body ready to perform optimally and safely.

Dynamic warm-ups, in particular, are vital for gymnastics because they mirror the activities performed during a session.

These routines involve movement-based stretching that warms up the muscles and increases range of motion and body awareness. For instance, arm circles, jumping jacks, and leg swings are fantastic for getting the heart rate up and the blood flowing.

These exercises incorporate expansive and engaging movements, helping to loosen up the body while making the warm-up fun and energetic. For younger gymnasts, transforming these movements into a game, such as pretending to be airplanes during arm circles or frogs during jumping jacks, can make the warm-up an exciting part of their gymnastics practice.

For different age groups, the structure of the warm-up can vary significantly. Younger children, for example, might have shorter attention spans and therefore benefit from quick, playful movements that keep them engaged. Incorporating imagery and play into their warm-ups keeps their interest alive and allows them to connect physically and mentally with the activities.

For older children or teens, their warm-up might also include more specific exercises that target areas of the body that will be particularly engaged during their gymnastic routines, like wrists and ankles, which are crucial for balancing and tumbling.

Consider setting small challenges or goals within the routine to make these warm-up exercises more engaging for all ages. This could be as simple as counting how many jumping jacks they can do in a minute or seeing how high they can kick during leg swings. Using a timer can add a sense of urgency and fun, turning these warm-ups into a friendly competition with themselves or with a sibling or parent.

Music also plays a fantastic role in enhancing engagement. Just like adults often enjoy workouts more with the right playlist, children can be motivated by energetic and uplifting music. It sets the pace and rhythm of the warm-up, making the session feel more like a dance party than a workout.

Another great tip is to involve the children in the planning of these routines. On different days, let them choose which warm-up exercises to do from a list of options. This ensures they are engaged and gives them a sense of ownership and responsibility for their practice. It teaches them from an early age the importance of warming up, and by making these decisions, they learn about their bodies and what they need to feel ready and safe to perform gymnastics.

Remember, the goal of these warm-up exercises isn't just to prevent physical injuries; it's also about preparing mentally for the session ahead. A good warm-up reduces the risk of performance anxiety and helps establish a focused, positive mindset.

Whether it's through dynamic stretches, playful games, or challenges, each warm-up session is an opportunity to set the tone for a productive and enjoyable gymnastics practice. By incorporating these elements, you ensure that your child stays safe and grows in their love and enthusiasm for gymnastics, keeping each session lively and something they look forward to.

1.5 The Importance of Stretching: Techniques and Benefits

If you've ever watched a cat wake up from a nap, you've noticed it naturally stretches before doing anything else. This instinctive act, often overlooked in our daily routines, is crucial in gymnastics, where flexibility and the range of motion are paramount.

Stretching enhances these aspects and significantly lowers the risk of injuries. When muscles are well-stretched, they are less prone to tearing under strain during more dynamic movements like flips or vaults. Moreover, for a gymnast, the ability to stretch effectively can dramatically improve performance by allowing more fluid, precise, and higher-range movements.

Let's delve into the various stretching techniques beneficial for gymnasts, focusing primarily on static and dynamic stretches. Static stretching involves holding a stretch in a challenging but comfortable position for a period of time, usually between 15 to 30 seconds. This type of stretching is best performed after a workout when the muscles are warm and pliable.

For example, a simple toe touch, where one stands with feet together and bends forward to reach the toes, is a static stretch that targets the hamstrings, a crucial muscle group for many gymnastics movements.

On the other hand, dynamic stretching involves moving parts of your body and gradually increasing reach, speed of movement, or both. This type of stretching is ideal before starting a gymnastics session as it helps increase blood flow and muscle temperature, enhancing performance and decreasing the risk of injuries. Leg swings, arm circles, and gentle twists are examples of dynamic stretches that prepare the body for the vigorous activities inherent in gymnastics.

Integrating these stretching routines into a daily gymnastics practice is not just about performing them; it's about making them a seamless part of the workout. A good rule of thumb is to start with dynamic stretches to warm up the body, followed by the gymnastics workout, and then finish with static stretches to cool down the muscles and improve flexibility over time. This routine helps in maintaining a balance between strength and flexibility, which is vital for any gymnast.

For children of different ages, stretching needs to be approached differently. Younger children are naturally more flexible but may not have the patience for long static stretches. For them, dynamic stretches that involve playful movements can be more effective and engaging. Incorporating stories or themes, like pretending to be an animal reaching for food or swinging through trees, can make the experience fun and interactive.

As children grow older and their gymnastics skills advance, they can be gradually introduced to more structured static stretches. It is crucial to ensure that these stretches are done correctly to avoid strain or injury. Encouraging kids to focus on the feeling of the stretch rather than trying to reach a particular position helps them better understand their body's limits and capabilities.

Remember, stretching is not just a routine but a fundamental aspect of gymnastics that ensures safety, enhances flexibility, and improves overall performance. By making stretching an integral and enjoyable part of your gymnastics practice at home, you're setting a foundation for your child's success in the sport. It prepares their bodies for the challenges of gymnastics and instills a habit that benefits their general well-being and physical health far beyond the mat.

1.6 Creating a Weekly Gymnastics Schedule for Different Age Groups

Establishing a routine that nurtures your child's enthusiasm for gymnastics while keeping their weekly agenda balanced is like crafting a recipe; it requires a mix of ingredients such as time for practice, rest, and other activities. The key is to set realistic and achievable goals that align with your child's age, ability, and interest, ensuring they remain motivated and enjoy their gymnastics practice without feeling overwhelmed.

When setting goals, it's important to consider what is developmentally appropriate for each age group. For younger children, ages five to eight, focus on simple, fun, and short-term goals like mastering a forward roll or balancing on one foot for a few seconds. These goals are easily attainable, which helps boost their confidence and eagerness to engage in practice sessions.

For older children, ages nine to 12, you can set more challenging goals that require a bit more persistence, such as achieving a perfect cartwheel or holding a handstand for more than a few seconds. These goals encourage perseverance and help improve their gymnastic skills more significantly.

Creating a sample weekly schedule can help distribute practice and rest periods effectively. For younger children, consider three practice sessions a week, each lasting about 30 minutes, followed by a short stretching session to help them wind down and prevent any potential strain.

Each session should begin with a dynamic warm-up, followed by practicing specific skills or routines, and conclude with a fun activity like a gymnastics-related game to keep their spirit high. On the other hand, older children might benefit from slightly longer sessions, say 45 minutes to an hour, four times a week, with each session structured to warm up, skill practice, and a cool-down period that includes more extensive stretching to cater to their enhanced endurance and concentration levels.

The adaptability of the schedule based on the child's progress and interest is crucial. Regularly assess your child's engagement and progress, and be ready to adjust the schedule accordingly. If they seem to be losing interest, reducing the frequency of practices or incorporating more varied and fun activities might be helpful.

Conversely, if they are particularly enthusiastic and progressing well, you might consider gradually increasing the challenge of the skills practiced or the duration of the sessions. Always keep an open dialogue with your child to ensure the schedule aligns with their feelings and preferences.

Balancing gymnastics with other activities is essential for well-rounded development. Gymnastics should be part of a broader set of activities that stimulate different aspects of growth in your child. For instance, if your child also enjoys drawing or playing a musical instrument, allocate time during the week for these activities too.

This prevents burnout from too much physical exertion and nurtures their mental and creative faculties. Planning a balanced week might look like alternating gymnastics practice days with days dedicated to other interests or setting aside weekends for family outings and rest. Remember, the ultimate aim is to support your child's growth and passion for gymnastics while ensuring they lead a balanced and joyful life.

This balanced approach helps nurture a healthy routine where gymnastics becomes a beloved part of their week, eagerly anticipated rather than viewed as a chore. By fostering this positive attitude toward regular practice and balancing it with leisure and rest, you set the foundation for good gymnastics skills and a lifetime of healthy habits.

Navigating the creation of a gymnastics schedule for your child involves understanding their needs, encouraging their interests, and being flexible enough to adjust as they grow and their abilities evolve. Whether your child is just beginning to explore gymnastics or has been flipping around the living room for years, a well-thought-out schedule is your roadmap to supporting them in a structured yet enjoyable way.

As you both enjoy this process, remember that each step, each little achievement, builds towards greater confidence and skill, enriching your child's experience not just in gymnastics but in life itself.

TWO

Fundamental Gymnastics Skills

I magine your child, full of energy and enthusiasm, ready to learn the basics of gymnastics right in your living room. It's not just about the flips and jumps; it's about building a solid foundation with basic skills that ensure safety and promote an understanding of body mechanics.

One of the first and most crucial skills in gymnastics is rolling. Rolling teaches body awareness, coordination, and, importantly, how to fall safely. In this chapter, we dive into the intricacies of rolling techniques, providing you with detailed guidance to help your child roll safely and effectively.

2.1 Rolling Techniques: Forward, Backward, and Sideways

Understanding the Mechanics

Rolling may seem simple, but it involves precise body mechanics that are crucial for executing the move safely and efficiently. Let's break down each type of roll:

- **Forward Roll**: The forward roll begins with a crouch, hands placed flat on the mat slightly in front of the feet. As your child tucks their head and pushes off with their legs, their back rounds, and they roll forward. The neck must remain tucked to avoid placing any weight directly on the head; instead, the roll should progress from the shoulders down the back smoothly.
- **Backward Roll**: This roll starts from a seated position with legs bent and hands placed beside the ears on the mat. Pushing off from the legs, your child will roll over the shoulders (not the neck) onto the upper back and return to a seated or standing position. Much like the forward roll, the key is maintaining a rounded back to ensure a smooth rolling motion.
- **Sideways Roll**: The sideways roll is often overlooked, but it's excellent for developing lateral movement skills. Starting from a seated position, your child will lean to one side, placing their arm down as they roll over the side of their hip and back, transitioning smoothly from one side of the body to the other.

Step-by-Step Instruction

For each roll, it's important to follow these detailed, sequential instructions to ensure your child performs them safely:

1. **Setup**: Start in the correct initial position for each roll (crouch for forward, seated for backward, and side-seated for sideways).
2. **Initiation**: Engage the core and prepare to push off. Forward and backward rolls involve a slight push from the legs. For sideways rolls, the side of the body leads the movement.

3. **Execution**: Roll smoothly, maintaining a tight tuck of the head (forward and backward rolls) or side curve (sideways roll). The arms help guide the movement and protect the head and neck.

4. **Completion**: End each roll in a controlled manner— standing up from a forward roll, sitting up from a backward roll, and transitioning sides for a sideways roll.

Common Mistakes and Corrections

Beginners often make a few common errors when learning how to roll:

- **Improper Head Positioning**: A common mistake is not tucking the chin enough, which can cause the head to contact the ground. Correcting this involves practicing the chin-to-chest motion separately before attempting rolls.
- **Insufficient Momentum**: Not pushing off enough can halt the roll midway. Practice gentle pushes in the initial position to get a feel for the required momentum.
- **Uncontrolled Movement**: Rolling too fast or unevenly can lead to disorientation or improper landings. Encourage slow, controlled movements initially to build muscle memory.

Practice Drills

To reinforce these techniques, here are some simple drills:

- **Roll Over an Obstacle**: Place a soft, low obstacle like a rolled-up towel on the mat. Have your child practice forward rolls over it to encourage proper tucking and rolling techniques.

- **Partner Rolls**: Pair up with your child to guide them through the motion. Support their back in forward rolls and hips in backward rolls to ensure they feel the correct movement pattern.
- **Marked Path Rolls**: Use tape to create a straight line on the mat. Have your child try to follow the line while rolling to improve directional control.

Rolling is a fundamental skill that sets the stage for more complex gymnastics movements. By mastering forward, backward, and sideways rolls, your child enhances their gymnastic ability and learns crucial skills in body awareness and safe falling. These are not just techniques but building blocks for confidence and safety in all physical activities.

2.2 Introduction to Handstands: Preparation and Safety

Handstands, a fundamental skill in gymnastics, thrill spectators and offer numerous benefits to the gymnast, including increased upper body strength, balance, and spatial awareness. As we begin to explore the world of handstands, let's first ensure that your child is building the right muscle strength and mastering the safety techniques to make every attempt at a handstand both fun and safe.

Preparatory Exercises

Building the strength for handstands is like preparing to build a house; the foundation must be solid for everything else to hold up. Focus initially on strengthening the arms, shoulders, and core, as these body parts play a crucial role in maintaining the handstand. Exercises such as 'planks' and 'push-ups' are excellent for building arm and shoulder strength.

Even simple activities like hanging from a bar can significantly improve grip and arm strength. Exercises like 'sit-ups' or 'V-ups' are incredibly effective for core strengthening. These exercises prepare the muscles for the exertion of doing a handstand and help maintain balance and stability once your child is upside-down.

Progression Steps

Starting with basic skills and gradually moving to more complex ones ensures a safe learning curve and helps build confidence. Begin with wall-assisted handstands, which are an excellent way for beginners to feel what being upside-down is like without worrying about balancing.

Have your child face away from the wall, place their hands on the floor, and walk their feet up the wall until their body is in a straight line. This position should be held for a few seconds to build endurance.

As their confidence grows, encourage them to kick up against the wall with their backs facing it, which more closely mimics a free-standing handstand. The final step in this progression is the free-standing handstand, starting with short bursts of balancing without support and gradually increasing the duration as strength and skill improve.

Safety Measures

Safety must be a top priority when practicing handstands. Always ensure there's a spotter—either yourself or an older sibling—who can guide and support your child as they practice. When transitioning from wall-assisted to free-standing handstands, a spotter provides the necessary safety net to prevent falls and injuries.

Additionally, practice on a soft, padded surface. Gymnastics mats are ideal, as they offer cushioning in case of falls. If a professional mat is not available, a thick, soft blanket or a pile of carpets can also temporarily serve the purpose. Make sure the area around the practice space is clear of any objects or furniture to avoid injuries.

Troubleshooting Common Challenges

Balance maintenance and wrist strain are common challenges when learning handstands. For balance issues, exercises like 'frog stands' or 'headstands' can help your child develop a better sense of balance in an inverted position. These exercises are less intensive than full handstands but provide a good intermediary step for balance training.

Wrist strain can be mitigated by proper warm-up and strengthening exercises for the wrists. Encourage your child to do wrist rolls and stretches both before and after practice to keep the wrists flexible and strong. They can also use wrist guards or wraps for extra support and strain prevention during practice.

By following these detailed steps and focusing on gradual progression, safety, and troubleshooting common issues, your child will be equipped to safely enjoy learning handstands. This skill enhances their gymnastics capabilities and contributes to their overall physical fitness and confidence. Remember, patience and consistent practice are key in mastering handstands, just like any other gymnastic skill.

2.3 The Art of Cartwheeling: A Guide for First-Timers

The cartwheel, an iconic gymnastic movement, captures the essence of fluid motion and control, transforming the body into a revolving figure that resembles the spokes of a wheel in motion. For young gymnasts, mastering the cartwheel is a milestone in their gymnastic development and a fundamental skill that enhances coordination, balance, and body awareness.

Let's dive into the key positions and steps involved in performing a cartwheel, ensuring your child understands and executes this dynamic move with grace and safety.

Fundamental Positions

The beauty of a cartwheel begins with its foundational positions, each critical for the smooth execution of the entire movement. It starts with the **lunge position**, where one foot steps forward, knees slightly bent, and arms extended straight upwards, framing the ears. This starting stance is crucial as it sets the direction and provides the momentum necessary for the cartwheel.

Next, as the body inverts, it passes through the **star position**—a moment where the body is ideally horizontal to the ground, balanced on the hands, with legs and arms stretched out straight, forming a wide 'X' shape. This position is not just about aesthetics; it emphasizes the importance of maintaining a straight line from hand to hand and toe to toe, which is key to achieving a balanced and controlled rotation.

The final phase of the cartwheel is the **landing**, which ideally mirrors the initial lunge but with the opposite foot forward, demonstrating a successful rotational symmetry.

Instructional Steps

Executing a cartwheel requires a fluid connection of movements, each flowing into the next without hesitation. Here's how you can guide your child through these steps:

1. **Initiate from the Lunge**: From the initial lunge position, with the dominant leg forward, instruct your child to lean forward, transferring their body weight onto the front leg, and begin to tip forward, placing the hands on the ground one at a time.
2. **Hand Placement and Rotation**: The first hand to touch the ground should be the one opposite the front leg. As the body begins to invert, the second hand comes down to mirror the first, effectively creating a brief handstand phase. It's imperative that the hands are firmly planted and shoulder-width apart to support the body's weight during rotation.
3. **Kick Over**: With hands securely on the ground, the back leg (the one opposite to the leading hand) kicks up first, driving the rotation, followed by the leading leg.

Both legs should remain straight and split apart, reaching for the star position.

4. **Land and Finish**: As the rotation completes, the legs come down in reverse order of the initial lunge. The first leg to land should be the one that kicked off last, followed by the initial front leg, ending in a lunge that mirrors the start.

Visualization Techniques

Visual aids and metaphors can be incredibly effective in helping your child grasp the flow of a cartwheel. Imagine the body moving like the hands of a clock, with the head and feet tracing the circle's circumference. You can also use a drawn arc on a piece of paper to show the path each hand and foot should take, helping them visualize the movement simply and understandably. Sometimes, demonstrating a slow-motion cartwheel yourself or showing a video can also provide a clear model for them to emulate.

Practice Tips

Consistent practice is key to refining the technique and building the confidence necessary for a smooth cartwheel. Here are some tips to ensure effective practice sessions:

- **Use Soft Mats**: Practice on soft mats to cushion falls and build confidence without the fear of getting hurt.
- **Spotting**: Initially, assist your child by supporting their hips during the rotation and guiding them through the motion until they feel confident executing it unaided.

- **Repetition and Feedback**: Encourage repeated practice by gently correcting form and technique after each attempt. Positive reinforcement helps build enthusiasm and persistence.
- **Safety First**: Always ensure the practice area is clear of obstacles, and teach your child to stop and reset if they feel off-balance or unsure at any step of the process.

By breaking down the cartwheel into manageable steps, using visual tools for better understanding, and encouraging regular, safe practice, your child will not only master the cartwheel but also develop a deeper appreciation for the art of gymnastics.

While challenging at the outset, this skill opens the door to more complex techniques and routines, enriching your child's gymnastic journey with each turn and tumble.

2.4 Mastering the Bridge and Backend: Tips for Flexibility

Flexibility is not just about being able to bend and twist in extraordinary ways; it's a fundamental aspect of gymnastics that can significantly enhance performance while reducing the risk of injuries. The bridge and backbend are iconic gymnastics skills and vital exercises to boost the flexibility of the back and shoulders. These movements stretch and strengthen the spine, shoulders, and hip flexors, which are crucial for almost every gymnastic skill.

To begin working on back and shoulder flexibility, your child can engage in several preparatory exercises. Start with simple stretches like the cat-cow, where they alternate between arching their back towards the ceiling and dipping it towards the floor. This exercise warms up the spine and introduces gentle movement.

For shoulder flexibility, arm circles are effective and can be fun for kids as they pretend to draw big and small circles with their hands. Incorporating yoga poses such as the cobra, where one lies on the stomach and lifts the chest off the ground using the back muscles, can also be incredibly beneficial. These exercises should be performed regularly, as part of gymnastics practice and as a routine to maintain and improve flexibility.

When your child is ready to attempt the bridge, ensure they start with a proper warm-up focusing on the spine and shoulders. They should start by lying on a mat, knees bent, and feet flat on the floor, close to the buttocks. Hands should be placed on the floor beside the head, fingers pointing towards the shoulders. This setup is crucial as it forms the foundation of a safe and effective bridge.

The next step is to lift the hips towards the ceiling, followed by the back, and finally, push the hands and feet onto the floor to lift the entire body off the ground. The hips must be lifted high enough to form a straight line from the shoulders to the knees, avoiding unnecessary strain on the back. Encourage your child to hold the bridge position for a few seconds initially, gradually increasing the duration as they become more comfortable and strong in the pose.

As always, safety and proper alignment are paramount during this exercise. The hips, shoulders, and head must be aligned to prevent undue pressure on the spine. A common mistake is to let the head fall back too far, which can strain the neck. Teach your child to keep their eyes looking back towards their hands, which helps maintain the correct head position.

Another frequent issue is sagging hips, which can be corrected by strengthening the core muscles. Regular practice of the bridge will naturally improve these aspects. Still, it's crucial to keep an eye on these common form errors and correct them early.

Modifications can be made to simplify the bridge for beginners or those with limited flexibility. One effective modification is to use an elevated surface, such as a gymnastics block or a sturdy cushion, to support the back. This reduces the angle of the bridge and the flexibility required to perform it.

Another option is to practice the bridge against a wall, where your child can walk their hands down the wall into the bridge position. This method allows them to control the depth of the backbend gradually and increases confidence in the movement. Just make sure you're spotting them in case their hands slip.

Regularly practicing these flexibility exercises and the bridge can significantly enhance your child's gymnastic abilities. Not only do they improve the range of motion, but they also contribute to the overall development of body control and strength, essential elements in gymnastics.

As your child progresses, these foundational skills will support them in learning more complex movements and building a robust gymnastic skill set rooted in safety, flexibility, and fun.

2.5 Jumping and Landing: How to Do It Safely

When it comes to gymnastics, the ability to jump high and land safely is not just impressive; it's essential. Jumping is a dynamic skill that serves as a foundation for many gymnastics routines, while safe landing techniques prevent injuries and ensure longevity in the sport.

Here, we'll explore how you can help your child develop the power and technique needed for effective jumping and the critical skills necessary for safe landings.

Jumping Techniques

Jumping might seem simple—bend your knees and push off, right? However, effective jumping in gymnastics requires a bit more finesse and a lot of practice. It begins with a solid base: the stance. Teach your child to start with their feet shoulder-width apart, which provides balance and stability.

From this position, the next step involves what we call the 'pre-load' phase, where the gymnast bends their knees and lowers their body into a squatting position. This action is important, as it builds the potential energy required for the jump. The arms also play a vital role; they should swing back during the squat and then forcefully come upward during the jump, adding momentum and height.

The explosive phase of the jump is next. This is where your child will extend their legs, push off the ground with their feet, and use the swing of their arms to lift their body upwards. It's essential to emphasize pushing the floor away with the balls of the feet, which engages the leg muscles fully and adds to the jump's height and power. Encouraging your child to imagine jumping over a high object or reaching for the sky can help them maximize their effort during this phase.

Landing Mechanics

Now, what goes up must come down; in gymnastics, how you come down is just as important as how you go up. Proper landing technique is vital to absorb the impact and reduce the strain on the body, particularly on the joints. The key to a safe landing is to make it as soft as possible.

Teach your child to always land with their knees slightly bent. This action helps absorb the impact, reducing the force transmitted through the legs and spine. Their feet should be about hip-width apart to maintain balance, and the toes should be pointing forward.

The role of the arms continues even when landing. After helping to propel the body upwards, they should be ready to help stabilize the body as it comes down. Instruct your child to reach forward with their arms as they land, which helps maintain balance and control. The chest should be upright, and the gaze forward, ensuring that the body doesn't lean too far forward or backward, which can lead to falls or undue stress on the back.

Drills for Practice

To reinforce these jumping and landing techniques, simple drills can be very effective. Start with basic vertical jumps, where your child focuses solely on the mechanics of jumping and landing as described. Once they are comfortable with this, introduce targets to reach with their hands when they jump, which encourages them to jump higher and keeps the activity fun and engaging.

Box jumps, which progress from vertical jumps, are an excellent way to practice both the jump and the landing. Use a soft, low box or step initially. Your child should stand in front of the box, perform the jump onto the box with both feet landing softly, and then step down again. As their confidence and skill increase, the height of the box can be gradually increased.

Incorporating Jumps into Routines

As your child becomes more proficient in jumping and landing, these skills can be integrated into simple gymnastics routines. A basic routine might involve a sequence of a vertical jump, a pivot turn, and then a jump off a small platform or beam. Not only does this help in applying the skills in a more realistic gymnastics context, but it also aids in developing their routine execution and overall athletic performance.

By focusing on the fundamental techniques of jumping and landing, you provide your child with the tools they need to perform these movements safely and effectively. This enhances their gymnastics capabilities and contributes to their overall physical development, coordination, and enjoyment of the sport. Remember, patience and consistent practice are key, as these foundational skills take time to develop but are essential for any aspiring gymnast.

2.6 Balancing Skills: Fun Exercises on the Beam

Introducing your child to the balance beam might just be one of the most thrilling parts of their early gymnastics experiences at home. The balance beam, even at a basic level, teaches precision, control, and, of course, balance—all essential skills for a budding gymnast.

For home use, you have a few options that can fit different spaces and safety concerns. Foam beams are fantastic for beginners; they're soft, low to the ground, and reduce the risk of injuries from falls. As confidence and skills grow, you might consider a low wooden beam, which offers a more realistic feel but still keeps the risk low due to its proximity to the floor.

Starting with some simple balancing exercises can make beam work fun and engaging. Walking forward on the beam is a great beginning exercise. Encourage your child to take slow, heel-to-toe steps, focusing on keeping their arms extended to the sides for balance.

As they gain confidence, challenge them to walk backward or sideways. These variations keep the practice exciting and enhance their spatial awareness and agility. For a bit more fun, turn these walking exercises into a game by timing how long they can stay on the beam without stepping off or see how many steps they can take in a given time frame.

Another engaging exercise is the 'beam dance,' where you create a simple sequence of movements for your child to perform on the beam—like spinning, hopping on one foot, or even kneeling and standing up.

This improves their physical balance and helps them develop cognitive skills as they remember and execute the sequence. You can make this more challenging and interactive by playing music and having them move to the rhythm, adding timing and coordination to the balance training.

A simple chart can be effective in keeping track of your child's progress on the beam. Each day of practice, they can add a sticker or mark off what skills were practiced and how well they performed. This helps track progress over days and weeks and boosts motivation as they see their improvements visually.

Additionally, setting small, achievable goals each week, such as 'walk across the beam ten times without faltering' or 'perform the beam dance for 30 seconds longer than last time,' gives them clear objectives to strive for, making each practice session purposeful.

Safety on the balance beam, even a low one, is paramount. Always ensure the beam is set up in an area free of obstacles that could cause injury if your child falls. Using safety mats around the beam can provide a soft landing spot, easing the fear of falling and reducing the risk of injury.

It's also important to teach proper dismount techniques from the start. A simple step-off the beam is safest for beginners. As your child becomes more experienced and confident, they can learn more complex dismounts, but always under close supervision to ensure they are performed safely.

Incorporating these fun and varied exercises on the balance beam keeps your child engaged and enjoying their gymnastics practice and builds foundational skills vital for more advanced gymnastics techniques. By tracking their progress and ensuring their safety, you help create a supportive environment that encourages consistent practice and improvement, setting the stage for a fulfilling and successful gymnastics experience at home.

This exploration of balancing skills wraps up our journey through fundamental gymnastics skills, equipping your child with the basics they need to enjoy and succeed in this dynamic sport. As we move forward, the next chapter will delve into more specialized gymnastics techniques, helping your child continue to grow and refine their abilities in this exciting athletic discipline.

THREE

Progressing in Gymnastics

A s your child's confidence grows and their foundational skills in gymnastics become more solid, it's thrilling to think about what comes next. One of the most visually striking and fun gymnastics skills to learn is handstand walking.

It's not just about standing upside down; it's about moving dynamically in that inverted position, which combines strength, balance, and a bit of daring. This next step in your child's gymnastics adventure builds physical prowess, mental resilience, and determination.

3.1 Handstand Skills: Moving Toward Handstand Walking

Building on Fundamentals

Before your young gymnast starts their first steps on their hands, it's crucial to ensure they have a solid grasp of a basic handstand. The foundational handstand sets the stage for more advanced moves and teaches balance and body alignment skills.

In a basic handstand, the body must form a straight line from the hands through the arms and torso, all the way to the toes. This alignment guarantees the body's weight is supported correctly and balanced. You can practice this with your child by having them perform handstands against a wall.

Encourage them to focus on tightening their core, aligning their body, and breathing evenly. This practice helps in building muscle memory and confidence, which are essential when transitioning to walking on hands.

Step-by-Step Guidance to Handstand Walking

Transitioning from a static handstand to walking on hands can seem challenging at first, but with patience and practice, it becomes an exhilarating skill for kids to master. Start by gently prompting your child to shift their weight from one hand to the other while in the basic handstand position. This weight shifting is the fundamental principle behind handstand walking.

Once they feel comfortable with shifting their weight, the next step is to attempt small 'steps' with their hands. These steps should be short and controlled initially, focusing on maintaining balance and body alignment. Practicing in a hallway or against a long wall can provide your child with guidance and a sense of security as they learn this new skill.

Strength and Stability Workouts

A gymnast needs a strong upper body and a stable core to effectively walk on their hands. Exercises that improve shoulder strength and core stability are key. Activities like push-ups, pike presses, and plank walks are incredibly beneficial for shoulder strength. These exercises build the endurance and strength needed to support the body's weight during handstand walking.

For core stability, practices such as planks, hollow body holds, and leg raises help develop a powerful, stable midsection. Integrating these exercises into your child's regular training sessions not only aids in their overall gymnastics performance but specifically enhances their ability to perform handstand walking with control and confidence.

Practice Drills and Progress Tracking

Structured drills can significantly improve the learning curve for handstand walking. One effective drill is the 'wall crawl,' where your child starts in a handstand with their feet against the wall and gradually walks their hands away from the wall, trying to maintain the handstand as long as possible without wall support.

Another helpful drill is the 'handstand obstacle course,' which can be fun and challenging. Set up soft obstacles your child has to navigate while on their hands, enhancing their agility and control in the handstand walking.

To track progress, maintain a simple logbook or chart where your child can record how many steps they take or how long they can hold the handstand walk each session. Watching their progress visually can be a huge motivational boost and a fun way to see how far they've come.

Handstand walking is not just about physical skill; it's a fun and engaging way for your child to challenge themselves and see their abilities. Like any gymnastic skill, it requires practice, patience, and persistence, but the rewards—both in physical prowess and sheer joy—are immense.

As they lift their feet off the ground and balance the world on their palms, they're not just learning to walk on their hands but to turn the world upside down with confidence.

3.2 Round-off Skills: Connecting Cartwheels to Round-offs

When your child has mastered the cartwheel, the excitement of progressing to round-offs begins. Unlike the cartwheel, where the body finishes in the same direction it started, a round-off ends with the gymnast facing the opposite direction.

This dynamic skill is a cornerstone in gymnastics routines and a thrilling challenge that enhances agility, coordination, and power. Understanding the technical nuances of a round-off can significantly impact your child's ability to perform it successfully and safely.

The round-off starts similarly to a cartwheel, but the magic lies in the strong push-off and the twist of the body mid-air. As your child begins the round-off, they will enter a hurdle step—a preparatory movement where they gain momentum by stepping into the cartwheel motion.

However, unlike a cartwheel, as their hands hit the ground, their legs snap together, and their hips twist, allowing them to land with both feet together, facing the opposite direction from where they started. This quick snapping and twisting are crucial as they convert the horizontal momentum into vertical, preparing them for subsequent skills like back handsprings or leaps.

For drills that enhance the transition from a cartwheel to a round-off, start with what I like to call 'half-round-offs.' Have your child perform a cartwheel, but ask them to try to land with their feet together. This drill focuses on the latter part of the movement, helping them get used to the feeling of twisting their hips and pulling their legs together before they land.

As they become more comfortable with this, you can introduce 'round-off rebounds,' where immediately after landing the round-off, your child performs a straight jump. This helps master the landing and builds the explosive power needed for more advanced tumbling sequences.

Common mistakes in learning round-offs often involve timing and body positioning. One typical error is the failure to fully snap the legs together and twist the hips before landing, which can result in an incomplete or unbalanced skill. To correct this, practice the 'snap and twist' drill, where your child focuses solely on the mid-air motion without the hurdle step.

They start from a kneeling position, hands on the ground, and practice snapping their legs together and twisting their hips to land on their feet, facing the opposite direction. This isolates the most critical part of the round-off, allowing your child to focus on perfecting this movement.

Incorporating round-offs into gymnastics routines provides a creative and effective way to link various skills. For example, a simple routine (once they've grown in their abilities) could involve a round-off followed by a back handspring, which flows naturally due to the backward momentum generated by the round-off.

Alternatively, for a floor routine, a round-off can be beautifully connected to a leap or a dance move, showcasing technical skill and artistic expression. When practicing these combinations, ensure your child performs on a soft mat and has enough space to execute the movements without restriction. Watching and correcting their form during these practices helps prevent the development of incorrect techniques and maintains a safe practice environment.

By focusing on the critical elements of the round-off and incorporating structured, fun drills into practice sessions, your child will not only master this exciting skill but also build a strong foundation for more complex gymnastic achievements. As they flip and twist through the air, landing with precision and confidence, they're not just learning gymnastics but embracing a sport that challenges their body and mind, fostering growth and resilience.

3.3 Safety Measures for Basic Flips

Flipping is an exhilarating aspect of gymnastics that captures the essence of the sport—power, precision, and grace. Before your child takes the leap into performing flips, it's crucial to ensure they are fully physically and mentally prepared.

The foundation for successful flips starts with a blend of strength, flexibility, and basic gymnastics skills like rolls and handstands, which prepare the body for the complex mechanics of flipping. Ensuring your child has mastered these elements reduces the risk of injury and sets them up for success.

Starting with the prerequisites, your child should exhibit strong core and lower body strength. These areas are essential as they provide the stability and power to propel the body through the air.

Additionally, a good sense of body awareness—understanding how to control their body while in motion—is crucial. This can be developed through less complex gymnastic movements that involve rotation and inversion, building up to the more dynamic requirement of flips.

It's also important that your child feels mentally ready; they should be excited and not fearful about attempting flips, as hesitation can lead to improper technique and injury.

Front flips and backflips require a safe environment—ideally, a gymnastics gym with proper mats and, if possible, a foam pit or a spotting belt. If you feel your child has developed enough strength to practice flipping, seek out a local gym with proper equipment and qualified teachers to help them learn. These and other more dangerous, advanced skills shouldn't be learned at home.

3.4 Developing Strength for Gymnastics: Key Exercises

When we think about gymnastics, it's easy to marvel at the grace and flexibility of the athletes. However, underlying those elegant performances is a core of solid strength that makes all those spectacular moves possible.

Strength training is necessary for improving performance and also for minimizing the risk of injuries. As your child's muscles become stronger, they provide better support for their joints, which is essential in a sport that demands a lot from the body.

The core, the body's powerhouse, is essential for almost every movement in gymnastics. A strong core stabilizes the body, allowing for improved posture and better execution of skills. Continue with exercises like planks and hollow body holds, even as your young gymnast masters more skills.

Planks can be varied in many ways to keep them engaging and challenging. For instance, side planks focus on the obliques, and adding movements like leg lifts can increase the intensity. Hollow body holds, where your child maintains a banana-like shape lying on their back, are particularly effective for gymnasts as they mimic the body position needed for skills like tumbling and jumps.

Leg strength is equally important, especially for jumping and tumbling events. Squats and lunges are excellent exercises that can be done with or without weights (young children generally shouldn't use weights). These moves strengthen the large muscle groups in the legs, such as the quadriceps, hamstrings, and glutes.

For a fun variation, try incorporating jump squats or lunge walks, which also improve explosive power—a critical component for vaulting and floor routines. Additionally, calf raises, which can be done anywhere, help strengthen the lower legs, improving stability and landing mechanics.

Upper body strength cannot be overlooked, as it's crucial for events like bars and vault. Exercises like push-ups and pull-ups increase arm and shoulder strength. If a standard push-up is too challenging initially, starting with modified versions on the knees or against a wall can help build strength gradually.

If you don't have access to the right equipment for pull-ups, activities like climbing on playground equipment can provide similar benefits. Regularly incorporating these exercises builds muscle and enhances endurance, which is vital for longer practice sessions and routines.

Strength training should be integrated thoughtfully into your child's regular gymnastics practice to avoid exhaustion and overtraining. A practical approach might be alternating the focus between gymnastics skills and strength training exercises.

For example, if one day focuses heavily on leg-based skills like jumps and tumblings, the next could focus more on core and upper body strength. This helps maintain a balanced training schedule that keeps the sessions interesting and productive without overwhelming your young gymnast.

Monitoring and adjusting these workouts is key to continual improvement and motivation. Keeping a workout journal can be a fun way for your child to track their progress and see their improvements over time. Note down specifics like the number of repetitions, the duration of holds, and any increases in weight or resistance used.

This record not only shows how far they've come but also helps in planning future workouts. If progress in certain areas seems slow, it might be an indicator to adjust the focus of the training or to consider if additional recovery time is needed. Regular check-ins about how they feel after workouts can also provide insights into whether the training intensity is appropriate or needs modification.

Through consistent and well-planned strength training, your child will gain physical strength and confidence in their ability to perform various gymnastic skills. This strength builds a foundation that supports their development as a gymnast, helping them execute more complex moves with greater ease and assurance. As they grow stronger, they also learn the importance of perseverance and dedication—qualities that will benefit them far beyond the gymnastics mat.

3.5 Flexibility for Gymnastics: Advanced Stretching Techniques

As your child progresses in gymnastics, it becomes increasingly important to boost their flexibility. Advanced stretching techniques, such as Proprioceptive Neuromuscular Facilitation (PNF) stretching and dynamic stretches, are crucial in developing the range of motion required for higher-level gymnastics skills.

PNF stretching, in particular, is a method that involves both stretching and contracting the muscle group being targeted. This type of stretching is highly effective because it facilitates a greater increase in flexibility and strength.

For instance, in a PNF stretch for the hamstrings, your child would lie on their back and raise one leg up. You or a coach would gently push the leg towards their head to stretch the hamstring. They would then push against the resistance for a few seconds, relax, and you would push the leg towards the head again, deepening the stretch. This method helps in making substantial improvements in flexibility.

Dynamic stretches, unlike static stretches, involve movement. These are particularly useful before practice sessions as they help warm the body while improving flexibility. Examples include leg swings, arm circles, and torso twists. These movements increase blood flow to the muscles and joints, reducing the risk of injuries during intense gymnastics routines.

Integrating dynamic stretches into your child's daily training prepares their muscles and joints for the stress of gymnastics. It improves their overall performance by enhancing fluidity and range of motion in their movements.

When it comes to advanced stretching, understanding and adhering to safety guidelines is paramount. Overstretching can lead to injuries such as muscle strains or ligament tears. Always ensure your child warms up with light aerobic activity and dynamic stretches before moving into more intense stretching routines. It's important to listen to their body and avoid pushing them into painful positions.

Encourage them to focus on maintaining a steady breath, which helps relax the muscles and deepen the stretch without forcing it. Additionally, make sure that stretches, especially advanced ones, are performed under supervision or with clear instructions to maintain the correct form and alignment, thus preventing improper techniques that could lead to injuries.

Incorporating flexibility training into daily practice is essential for a gymnast's development. One effective way to ensure that stretching becomes a routine part of their training is to set specific times for flexibility workouts, either as a warm-up before practice or as a cool-down afterward.

Another strategy is to integrate flexibility challenges into their weekly routines; for instance, setting goals for splits or backbends can be highly motivating. Rewarding progress in flexibility, just like achievements in strength or skill mastery, also reinforces its importance. Regularly including flexibility assessments can help track improvements and identify areas that need more focus, ensuring a balanced development in all aspects of gymnastics.

By elevating the role of flexibility in your child's gymnastics training, you enhance their ability to perform complex skills and contribute to their long-term health and performance in the sport. Advanced stretching techniques like PNF and dynamic stretches provide the tools to achieve higher flexibility levels, which is essential for advanced gymnastics.

With careful attention to safety and a consistent approach to training, your child can achieve remarkable flexibility, which is beneficial for gymnastics and overall physical fitness. As they continue to stretch and strengthen their bodies, their potential in gymnastics will similarly expand, opening up new opportunities for growth and achievement in the sport.

3.6 Combining Skills: Creating Simple Routines

When your child reaches a point where they can confidently perform individual gymnastics skills, stringing these moves into a cohesive routine becomes the next step. Creating a gymnastics routine isn't just about technical execution; it's about storytelling through movement, expressing a theme, or simply showcasing the gymnast's best skills in a sequence that looks fluid and effortless.

Here's how you can help your child build their very first gymnastics routine, focusing on the integration of skills they love and are confident performing.

Routine Construction Basics

The foundation of a good routine is a well-thought-out sequence that highlights your child's strengths and flows naturally from one move to the next. Start by listing all the skills your child can perform comfortably. Next, group these skills into categories based on their type, such as jumps, balances, and tumbling.

This categorization helps in understanding which skills naturally lead to others. For example, a cartwheel might flow well into a round-off, or a leap could follow a series of dance steps beautifully.

When constructing the routine, think of it as a story with a beginning, middle, and end. The opening could be something striking to catch attention, like a dramatic balance move or a powerful jump. The middle part of the routine should be smooth, maintaining momentum with a mix of skills that demonstrate flexibility, strength, and technique.

Finally, conclude with a strong finish, such as a well-executed trick or a perfectly landed dismount, that will leave a lasting impression.

Choreography Tips

Choreographing a technically sound and aesthetically pleasing routine can be as fun as it is challenging. Encourage your child to think creatively about how they move between skills. Utilize different levels and speeds to add interest—for instance, combining high leaps with low rolls or fast spins with slow, graceful balances.

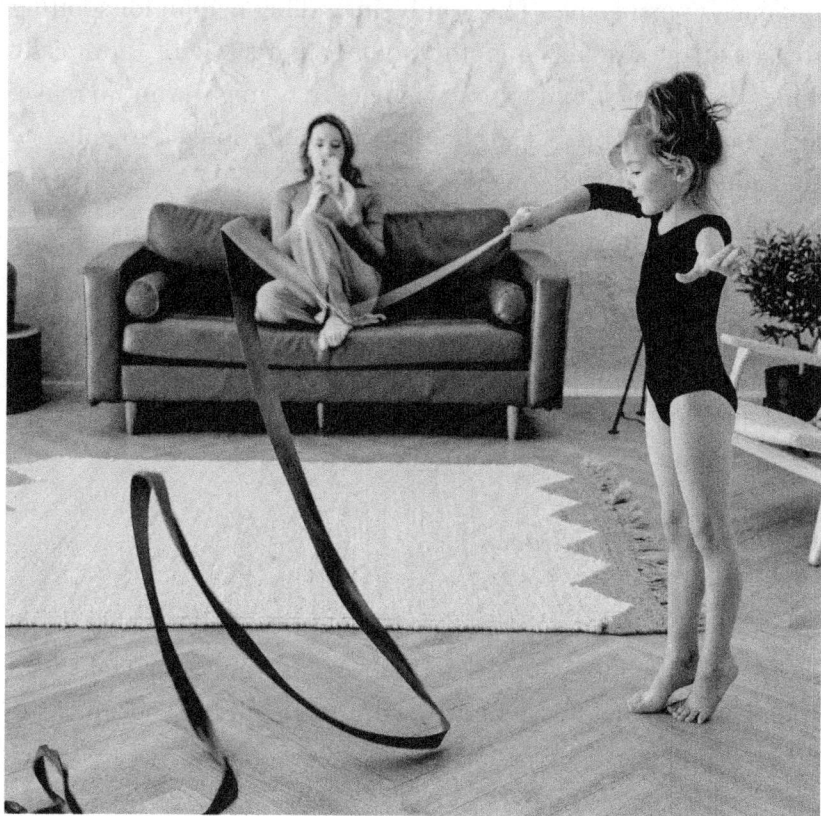

Music can play a vital role in choreography. Select a piece that inspires your child and matches the dynamic of the routine they want to perform. Music can guide the tempo and mood of the performance, making the choreography process more intuitive.

Practice Strategies

Practicing a gymnastics routine requires more than just physical repetition; it's about understanding the flow and rhythm of the performance.

One effective method is to use video playback. Recording practice sessions allows your child to see their performance from an audience's perspective. This can be incredibly helpful for spotting areas that need to be smoothed out or parts where they really shine. Encourage them to note changes they might want to make, such as tightening a pose or holding a balance longer, to enhance their routine's impact.

Additionally, segment the routine during practice sessions, focusing on perfecting small sections before stitching them together. This breakdown makes it less overwhelming and allows for detailed attention to the execution of each skill. Regularly mix these focused practices with full run-throughs to build stamina and maintain a sense of the routine's overall flow.

Performance Readiness

The final step before presenting a routine, whether in a casual showcase or a more formal setting, is ensuring your child feels confident and ready. Mental preparation is just as necessary as physical practice.

Discuss any performance anxieties they might have and help them develop strategies to manage nervousness, such as deep breathing or visualization techniques. Physically, confirm they are well-rested and have had a good warm-up before performing. A good warm-up prepares the body and mind, setting a positive tone for a confident performance.

Creating and performing a gymnastics routine is a wonderful journey for any young gymnast, allowing them to express their skills and creativity. It builds confidence in their gymnastics abilities and their capacity to perform and express themselves in front of others. They learn valuable lessons in persistence, artistic expression, and self-assurance as they plan, practice, and perfect their routine.

As this chapter closes, your child has the tools and knowledge to combine their gymnastics skills into beautiful, flowing routines. They've learned how to construct these routines, choreograph them creatively, practice effectively, and prepare mentally and physically for performance.

Next, we will explore more advanced gymnastics skills and techniques that can be integrated into these routines, continuing to challenge and excite young gymnasts as they grow in the sport.

FOUR

Gymnastics for Fitness and Fun

I magine transforming your backyard or living room into a playful circus ring, where laughter and cheers fill the air as your child dazzles with their newfound gymnastic skills. In this chapter, we dive into the world of gymnastics-themed games—a fantastic way to combine the thrill of learning gymnastics with the joy of play.

These games reinforce the skills your child has been mastering and put a healthy dose of fun into their routine, making each practice session something they eagerly look forward to. Whether it's a rainy day indoors or a sunny afternoon in the garden, these games are perfect for keeping your child engaged and active.

4.1 Gymnastics-Themed Games for Kids

Innovative Game Ideas

One of the most delightful ways to incorporate gymnastics into playtime is through gymnastics-themed games that challenge both the mind and body.

Let's start with "Gymnastics Tag"—a dynamic twist on the classic game of tag. In this version, the 'it' person must perform a gymnastic skill before they can tag someone else. For example, they might have to do three cartwheels or hold a handstand for five seconds. This game gets everyone moving and encourages kids to practice their skills under playful pressure.

Another great game is "Balance Beam Simon Says," which can be played on an actual beam or an imaginary line on the floor. The leader, or 'Simon,' commands the players to perform different actions on the beam, such as "Simon says, balance on one foot," or "Simon says, do a pivot turn." This game enhances balance and concentration, and the added element of following commands adds a cognitive challenge.

Benefits of Game-Based Learning

Integrating games into gymnastics practice has multiple benefits. First, it enhances motivation. Children, especially younger ones, may see repetitive drills as a chore. Games add excitement and variety, making learning enjoyable and something kids look forward to.

Moreover, games can reinforce skills and increase the retention of gymnastic techniques. When children practice a skill within the context of a game, they are more likely to execute it with more focus and effort, often without even realizing they are practicing.

Age-Appropriate Modifications

Ensuring these games suit various age groups and skill levels is crucial for safety and inclusivity. For younger children or beginners, the complexity of the skills in games like Gymnastics Tag can be reduced. Instead of a cartwheel, they might need to do a forward roll or a frog jump.

For older or more advanced gymnasts, increase the challenge by incorporating more complex skills or combining multiple skills. Always consider the physical environment as well—ensure there's enough space and the surface is safe for your planned activities.

Setup and Rules

Organizing these games is straightforward. For Gymnastics Tag, no special equipment is needed aside from a safe, open space. For Balance Beam Simon Says, if you don't have access to a balance beam, use a strip of tape on the floor.

Clearly explain the rules before starting, including any specific commands or skills to be used. It's also helpful to discuss the objectives of the game—to have fun and practice gymnastics skills in a fun way. This understanding can help maintain a positive and encouraging atmosphere focused on effort and enjoyment rather than just winning.

By transforming gymnastic drills into playful games, you keep your child's interest alive and deepen their love for the sport. These games provide a creative and engaging way to practice skills, improve physical fitness, and have a lot of fun along the way.

As children leap, balance, and tumble through these games, they enhance their gymnastic abilities and develop a lasting enthusiasm for physical activity.

4.2 Partner Activities: Enhancing Coordination and Teamwork

When two gymnasts come together to practice, they share a space and embark on a unique opportunity to enhance each other's skills through finely-tuned coordination and mutual trust. These partner activities, whether performed among peers or between a parent and child, can significantly enhance the learning experience. They introduce fun elements while doubling as an effective tool for improving gymnastic skills.

Partner Balance Exercises

One of the most engaging ways to develop balance and form is through partner balance exercises. Consider the 'mirrored posing,' where partners face each other, mimicking each other's movements as if one is the mirror image of the other.

This exercise enhances body awareness and requires each partner to maintain form and balance, adapting and reacting to the other's movements. It's a lively yet challenging activity that can be scaled in complexity depending on the participants' skill levels.

Another exciting exercise is the synchronized routine, where partners perform a sequence of gymnastics moves together. This could be as simple as simultaneous cartwheels or as complex as a choreographed sequence involving multiple types of skills. The key is maintaining the same timing and form, significantly enhancing coordination.

Trust-Building Activities

Trust is a foundational element in gymnastics where physical support can often be literal. Activities designed to build this trust are crucial, especially in a partner setting. 'Spotting drills,' where one partner supports or spots the other while they perform a potentially risky move like a back handspring, are vital. Not only do they ensure safety, but they also build a mutual assurance that each is there to support the other.

Another trust-building activity involves one partner guiding the other through an obstacle course while blindfolded, using only verbal instructions. This exercise emphasizes the importance of clear communication and trust in the partner's guidance, essential skills in gymnastics and everyday interactions.

Coordination Challenges

To spice up the gymnastics routine, introduce coordination challenges that require partners to work closely together. These can include exercises like dual walking on a balance beam, where each must adjust their steps and balance in response to the other, or partnered juggling with gymnastics ribbons, where each action needs to be perfectly timed to maintain the flow.

These challenges make the practice session more enjoyable and sharpen coordination skills, as each participant must constantly adjust their movements in sync with their partner.

Feedback Mechanisms

Finally, teaching partners how to provide constructive feedback to each other is invaluable. This skill fosters a supportive learning environment and encourages continuous improvement.

After each exercise, partners should discuss what went well and what could be improved, focusing on providing specific, actionable advice rather than general comments. This feedback loop helps refine skills and build a supportive rapport between partners, enhancing their teamwork and communication skills.

By integrating these partner activities into gymnastics practice, you enrich the training session with fun and challenging elements and foster an atmosphere of mutual respect and cooperation.

These exercises prepare young gymnasts not just for competitions or performances but for collaborative environments in all areas of life, teaching them the invaluable skills of trust, coordination, and constructive communication.

4.3 Fitness Challenges Using Gymnastics Skills

In the vibrant world of gymnastics, where each skill learned is a stepping stone to more remarkable achievements, introducing fitness challenges can be a compelling way to spice up the routine. These challenges provide a fun and engaging way for your child to apply their gymnastics skills and help them set and achieve new goals.

Picture setting up a timed obstacle course in your backyard, where each station requires a different gymnastic skill, such as a jump, a roll, or a balance. Your child dashes from one station to the next, their excitement palpable as they try to beat their previous time. This type of skill-based challenge not only tests their gymnastic abilities but also enhances their physical fitness and agility.

Tracking progress in these challenges can be both fun and motivational. Using a simple chart on the refrigerator door or a digital app specifically designed for tracking physical activity, your child can visually see their improvements. Whether it's faster completion times in an obstacle course, increasing the number of successful skill completions, or achieving higher scores in a routine, visible progress is a powerful motivator.

It encourages them to keep pushing their limits and reinforces the value of practice and perseverance. Each new achievement serves as a reminder of how far they've come and what they're capable of achieving next.

Adding a healthy level of competition to these challenges can further enhance their excitement and commitment. This could be as simple as setting up a friendly contest among siblings or friends, where each participant tries to outdo the others in a specific gymnastic challenge.

Alternatively, consider organizing a family gymnastics challenge where everyone participates and supports each other. These small group contests make the activities more engaging and encourage community and support, essential elements in maintaining long-term interest in any fitness regimen.

To make these challenges even more rewarding, consider implementing a reward and incentive system. For instance, achieving a personal best in a challenge could earn your child a badge or a certificate. Completing a tough challenge might be rewarded with a small prize, like a new piece of gymnastics equipment or an accessory.

Such rewards do more than just celebrate achievements; they reinforce the positive behaviors and efforts put into reaching those goals. They remind your child that hard work pays off, boosting their motivation to engage in and enjoy their gymnastics practice.

Through these fitness challenges, your child gets to showcase their gymnastics skills in fun and creative ways while also learning valuable lessons about setting goals, working toward them, and enjoying the rewards of their efforts.

They provide a dynamic platform for both physical and personal growth, where each leap and tumble is a step toward greater fitness and confidence.

4.4 Creative Movement: Combining Dance and Gymnastics

Integrating dance into gymnastics enhances the routines' aesthetic appeal and elevates the overall performance by improving fluidity, rhythm, and expressiveness. When gymnasts learn basic dance movements, they acquire new skills that complement their gymnastic techniques, allowing for more graceful and controlled movements.

Start by introducing fundamental dance steps that are easy to blend with gymnastic skills. For instance, ballet basics like pliés and pirouettes can improve balance and posture, which is essential for beam routines. Jazz steps such as kicks and leaps add dynamic energy to floor routines, making them more vibrant and exciting.

The beauty of combining dance with gymnastics lies in the endless possibilities for creativity. Choreography in gymnastics is not just about linking skills; it's about telling a story or conveying an emotion through movement. Even simple routines can be transformed into captivating performances with the right choreographic touch.

Begin by selecting a few gymnastic elements your child is comfortable with, such as handstands, rolls, or jumps. Next, think about how these elements can be artistically connected using dance movements. For instance, a forward roll can smoothly transition into a jazz slide, or a balance hold on the beam can be preceded by elegant ballet arm movements.

Creating choreography can be a fun and engaging process for young gymnasts. Encourage them to experiment with different movements and see how their gymnastic skills can be enhanced with dance. This exploratory approach helps develop a unique style and promotes a deeper understanding of body mechanics and movement dynamics.

When choreographing, keep the flow and timing of the routine in mind. Each movement should seamlessly lead into the next, maintaining a rhythm that matches the chosen music, which brings us to another crucial aspect of performance—music selection.

Music plays a pivotal role in gymnastics routines by setting the tempo and mood. Selecting the right music can amplify the impact of the performance, making it more powerful and dynamic. When choosing music for a gymnastics-dance routine, consider the rhythm, pace, and character of the piece.

The music should complement the movements with peaks and lulls that align with the intensity of the gymnastic elements. For younger gymnasts, choose music that is upbeat and simple, with a clear beat that is easy to follow. As they advance, more complex compositions that challenge their timing and expressiveness can be introduced.

Participating in local dance-gymnastics showcases or informal recitals provides a fantastic opportunity for young gymnasts to present their combined skills. These events allow them to experience the thrill of performance and to receive feedback from a broader audience.

Preparing for a showcase can significantly boost a gymnast's confidence and motivation, giving them a goal to work toward and a platform to celebrate their achievements. Invite your child to participate in these events, whether competitive or just for fun. The experience of performing in front of an audience teaches valuable lessons in stage presence, coping with nerves, and performing under pressure.

By embracing the fusion of dance and gymnastics, young gymnasts can enjoy a richer, more diverse training experience. This integration enhances their technical skills and encourages artistic expression, making each routine a unique and personal showcase of their talents.

As they continue to explore and combine these two beautiful forms of movement, they develop as athletes and performers, bringing creativity and passion to every leap, twirl, and flip.

4.5 Building Confidence Through Solo Performances

Developing a solo routine can be a transformative experience for young gymnasts, allowing them to put their skills and personal style on show. When guiding your child through the process of creating and refining a solo routine, focus on aligning the routine with their strengths and preferences, which can significantly boost their confidence.

To that end, start by selecting elements that your child performs well and enjoys, as this will make the routine more impressive and enjoyable for them to practice and perform. Encourage them to think creatively about how they can connect these elements in a way that feels smooth and natural.

This might involve transitioning from a series of jumps into a balance move or integrating a dance element to enhance the flow of the routine. The goal is to create a cohesive sequence that allows them to express their unique gymnastics flair.

As your child rehearses their routine, create a supportive environment where they feel safe to experiment and make mistakes. This is part of the learning process and helps them refine their performance. Offer constructive feedback on what they're doing well and areas where they could improve.

For example, if they're working on a floor routine, compliment their energy and suggest ways to tighten their form during jumps to increase their height and landing stability. Urge them to practice in front of a mirror or record their practice sessions so they can visually assess their performance, which can be incredibly effective in helping them understand how to improve.

The thought of performing solo in front of an audience can be daunting for many young gymnasts, leading to stage fright. To help your child manage nervousness, teach them techniques to boost their confidence and maintain focus.

Deep breathing exercises can be very effective as they help reduce anxiety and keep the mind clear. Practice these techniques together during rehearsals so they become a natural part of their pre-performance routine.

Visualization is another powerful tool. Teach your child to visualize their entire routine, seeing themselves execute each move flawlessly. This mental rehearsal can enhance their confidence and performance quality.

Promoting self-expression in their performances can also help young gymnasts connect more deeply with their routines. Help your child choose music they feel emotionally connected to, as this can significantly enhance their expression during the routine.

Discuss the story or emotions they wish to convey through their performance. Whether it's a tale of triumph, a display of joy, or an expression of their personal journey in gymnastics, this narrative can drive their performance, making it more engaging and heartfelt. Allow them to choose their costume and any props they might use, which can further personalize their routine and make the performance feel more authentic and self-expressive.

By focusing on these aspects—routine development, confidence in performing, self-assessment, and personal expression—you equip your child with the tools to succeed in their solo performances and enjoy them. They learn to see performances not just as challenges but as opportunities to express themselves and share their love for gymnastics.

Through this process, they gain physical skills and valuable life skills such as resilience, self-awareness, and the courage to stand in the spotlight and perform confidently.

4.6 Family Gymnastics Day: Activities for Everyone

Organizing a Family Gymnastics Day can be an excellent way to bring everyone together for fun, fitness, and bonding through the joy of movement. Whether in your backyard, at a local park, or even in a spacious living area, setting up a gymnastics day requires a bit of planning but results in a lot of laughter and cherished memories.

To start, you'll want to create a list of activities and a schedule that accommodates participants of all ages and skill levels. Include time for setup and breaks, especially if young children are involved, as they'll need time to rest and hydrate between activities.

When planning the activities, consider the space available and safety requirements. Simple equipment like mats for tumbling, a low beam for balancing exercises, and an area for free play can make the day enjoyable and safe for everyone.

Safety is paramount, so ensure all equipment is stable and appropriate for use and that the area is free of hazards. You might also want to have a first aid kit handy, just in case of minor scrapes or bruises.

Activities should cater to various skill levels and ages. For instance, you could set up a mini obstacle course that includes crawling under a string, hopping on a balance beam, and doing a forward roll on a mat.

You could incorporate more challenging skills like cartwheel contests or handstand competitions for older children or adults. Keep the activities light and fun; the goal is to enjoy the day without turning it into a serious competition.

Parents play a crucial role in this day—not only in ensuring safety and organization but also in participating and encouraging their children. Join in on the games, try some of the more straightforward gymnastic moves, and show your kids that gymnastics is fun at any age. This participation makes the activities more enjoyable for your children and strengthens the family bond as you all share in the effort and the laughs.

Capturing these moments on camera is another crucial aspect of Family Gymnastics Day. Photos and videos will be wonderful keepsakes and also help children see their progress and achievements. Create a photo challenge or a video diary of the day, encouraging everyone to take pictures or record each other trying different activities. At the end of the day, you can have a viewing party to relive the fun moments and celebrate everyone's efforts and achievements.

Organizing a Family Gymnastics Day is about more than just doing gymnastics; it's about creating an environment where every family member can try something new, challenge themselves, and, most importantly, have fun together. These shared experiences often leave lasting impressions, fostering a love for activity and a sense of closeness among family members.

As we wrap up this chapter, remember the joy and bonding that come from sharing these active moments. Engaging in gymnastics as a family promotes physical health and strengthens emotional connections, making every tumble and twirl a building block for lasting family memories.

Moving forward, the next chapter will delve into the mental aspect of gymnastics, which is every bit as important as the physical parts when exploring this dynamic sport.

Make a Difference with Your Review

UNLOCK THE POWER OF GENEROSITY

"The best way to find yourself is to lose yourself in the service of others."

Mahatma Gandhi

Helping others is one of the kindest things we can do. Not only does it make us happier, but it also makes the world a better place. While we're on this journey together, I hope you'll join me in making a difference.

Here's how you can help...

Would you lend a hand to someone you don't know, even if they never knew it was you?

Who is this person, you ask? They are just like you or your child. Maybe they're new to gymnastics, hoping to make a difference in their lives, and looking for guidance but unsure where to find it.

Our mission is to make gymnastics and physical activity accessible to every young person who is eager to learn. Everything we do stems from that mission. The only way for us to accomplish this is by reaching...well...everyone.

This is where you come in. Most people do judge a book by its cover (and its reviews). So, here's my request on behalf of a child who's eager to learn gymnastics but hasn't had the chance to join a class yet:

Please help that hopeful gymnast by leaving this book a review.

Your kind act won't cost a cent and takes less than 60 seconds, but it could change a child's life (and their parent's life) forever. Your review could help…

- …one more child to get physically active and improve their health.
- …one more parent to provide their little one with an activity they love, without becoming financially burdened.
- …one more child to reach their dream.

To feel good about making a real difference, all you have to do is…leave a review.

Simply scan the QR code to leave your review:

https://www.amazon.com/review/review-your-purchases/?asin=B0DDPZSYJ4

If you feel good about helping a young gymnast, you're my kind of person. Welcome to the club. You're one of us.

I'm that much more excited to help you learn gymnastics faster and easier than you can possibly imagine. You'll love the fun and exciting exercises I'm about to share in the coming chapters.

Thank you from the bottom of my heart. Now, back to our regularly scheduled tumbling fun!

- Your biggest fan, Josie Quaid

PS - Fun fact: When you help someone else, it makes you shine even brighter. If you think this book can help another aspiring gymnast, feel free to share it with them.

FIVE

Understanding the Mental Aspect of Gymnastics

I magine your child, eyes gleaming with determination, standing at the edge of the mat. They've been practicing a new routine for weeks; now, it's time for them to shine. As they step forward, there's a palpable mix of excitement and nerves. This moment is about more than just physical skill; it's a test of their mental prowess.

In gymnastics, the mental aspect can be just as demanding as the physical. It's not only about how well young athletes can move their bodies, but also about how effectively they can set goals, visualize success, and track their progress. This blend of mental activities can elevate their gymnastics from routine exercises to a dance of discipline and achievement.

5.1 Goal Setting Strategies for Young Gymnasts

Introduction to Goal Setting

Goals are the bridges that turn dreams into realities, especially in a sport as demanding as gymnastics. For young gymnasts, setting clear, achievable goals provides a roadmap to success. It gives them something tangible to strive toward and helps them gauge their progress.

It's like setting waypoints in a video game; reaching each one brings a sense of accomplishment and the thrill of moving closer to the ultimate prize. But these aren't just any goals; they must be tailored to fit each gymnast's aspirations and abilities, ensuring they're challenging yet reachable, pushing them to stretch their limits without straining their capabilities or dashing their hopes.

SMART Goals for Gymnasts

The SMART framework is a powerful tool for setting effective goals. It stands for Specific, Measurable, Achievable, Relevant, and Time-bound. Your child's goals in their gymnastics practice should pass the SMART test.

For example, instead of a vague goal like "get better at gymnastics," a SMART goal would be, "Learn to perform a clean round-off within the next three weeks." This goal is specific (focuses on the round-off), measurable (the performance can be observed and assessed), achievable (assuming the round-off is a skill within their reach with practice), relevant (improves their overall gymnastics routine), and time-bound (set for three weeks).

Using the SMART criteria transforms wishful thinking into actionable paths, making the journey in gymnastics explicit and directed.

Visualizing Success

We briefly mentioned visualization in the last chapter, but it's worth repeating here, as it's a valuable technique athletes use to enhance their performance. It requires conjuring up a detailed image of success in your mind before it happens, essentially practicing the sport in the mind's eye.

Teach your child to visualize themselves executing a perfect routine, feeling each movement in vivid detail, from the spring of the jump to the landing's satisfaction. This mental rehearsal can build confidence and reduce anxiety, as it familiarizes the gymnast with success, making it feel more attainable.

Encourage them to incorporate all senses in their visualization—imagining the feel of the mat under their feet, the sound of their breath, and even the smell of the chalk on their hands. This detailed imagery can make their mental practice as powerful as their physical practice.

Goal Tracking

Keeping track of progress toward goals is crucial in maintaining motivation and focus. Use a journal or a digital app designed for training to help your child record their daily activities and achievements.

This log should include what goals were set for the day, what was accomplished, and reflections on what worked and what didn't. Regular reviews of this journal can provide insightful feedback, helping adjust goals as needed and plan future sessions more effectively.

It also serves as a motivational tool, showing your child a concrete record of their progress and reminding them how far they've come. This tracking becomes a personal story of their gymnastics journey, filled with ups and downs, triumphs and lessons, continually guiding them toward their dreams.

In gymnastics, as in life, the mind can be a powerful ally or obstacle. By cultivating strong mental habits through effective goal setting, visualization, and progress tracking, you equip your child to succeed in gymnastics and apply these skills to any of life's arenas.

These mental disciplines help transform challenges into stepping stones to success, building a resilient and focused gymnast who approaches each routine with confidence and clarity.

5.2 Overcoming the Fear of Falling: Psychological Tips

The fear of falling is almost a rite of passage for many young gymnasts. It's a natural reaction to the challenging and sometimes dizzying heights and moves in gymnastics. Understanding this fear is the first step in helping your child manage it effectively.

Fear, especially in a sport like gymnastics, stems from worrying about physical injury or not performing up to expectations. It can manifest as nervousness before performing a routine or hesitation in trying out a new skill.

The psychological impact of this fear can be significant; it can hinder skill development and diminish the joy of gymnastics. Because of this, it's important to address the fear head-on, turning what could be a stumbling block into a stepping stone for confidence and success.

Cognitive-behavioral techniques are invaluable tools for managing fear effectively. These techniques involve reshaping the thought patterns that fuel fear.

For instance, positive self-talk can transform a child's mindset. Teach your child to replace thoughts like "I'm going to fall" with "I'm prepared, and I can do this." This kind of positive reinforcement helps build a mindset more focused on capability rather than fear.

Cognitive restructuring is another powerful technique. This involves challenging and changing the irrational beliefs that underpin fear. If your child believes that 'falling means failure,' guide them to understand that falling is a natural part of learning and improving in gymnastics, not a sign of failure.

Alongside cognitive strategies, physical relaxation techniques play a crucial role in managing the symptoms of fear. Techniques like deep breathing help in calming the mind and reducing the physical symptoms of anxiety, such as an increased heart rate or sweaty palms. Teach your child to take deep, slow breaths before they perform or when they feel scared.

Progressive muscle relaxation is another technique that can be beneficial. It involves tensing and then relaxing different muscle groups in the body. This helps reduce the tension built up due to fear and enhances bodily awareness, which is crucial in gymnastics.

Incremental exposure is a method that gradually introduces gymnasts to the elements that scare them in a controlled and supportive environment.

For instance, if a particular move on the high beam instills fear, the gymnast could start by practicing the move on a lower beam or a line on the floor. You can gradually increase the height as your child becomes more comfortable. This method allows your child to build confidence at their own pace and helps them realize they can manage and overcome their fear.

Combining these psychological and physical techniques creates a comprehensive strategy to help your child face and conquer their fear of falling. This approach improves their performance in gymnastics and empowers them with the skills to handle fears and challenges in other areas of their life.

Inspiring your child to embrace these techniques can transform their gymnastic practice into an empowering activity that they approach with confidence and excitement rather than apprehension and fear.

5.3 The Role of Focus and Concentration in Gymnastics

Maintaining sharp focus and concentration in gymnastics often sets good athletes apart from the truly great ones. Whether it's nailing a complex routine during a competition or mastering a new skill in practice, the mental clarity and focus required are immense.

Just as with physical skills, focus and concentration can be developed and enhanced through specific techniques and exercises, tailored to help young gymnasts hone their mental acuity alongside their physical prowess.

One effective technique to enhance focus is the practice of mindfulness. Mindfulness means being present in the given moment, tuning into your thoughts and sensations without judgment. For gymnasts, this can mean being acutely aware of each muscle movement and the rhythm of their breathing, all without letting the mind wander to past mistakes or future anxieties.

Invite your youngster to try mindfulness during warm-ups or cool-downs by focusing on deep, rhythmic breathing and visualizing each part of their body, acknowledging how it feels without attempting to change anything. This practice improves concentration and helps reduce performance anxiety, making them more present during their routines.

Minimizing distractions in the training environment is also crucial for maintaining focus. This can be as simple as keeping the practice area tidy and free of unnecessary equipment or as involved as setting specific 'quiet hours' in the gym where only essential communication is allowed.

At home, ensure that the practice space is isolated from noisy household activities and consider using 'Do Not Disturb' signs during practice sessions. Encouraging your child to keep a routine of tidying up their practice space before starting can also help minimize physical distractions and mentally cue them to focus on the session ahead.

The role of a consistent pre-performance routine cannot be overstated in its ability to boost concentration and performance under pressure. This routine should include physical warm-ups and mental preparation tactics such as visualization and affirmations.

For example, your child can develop a routine where they visualize executing a perfect routine from start to finish, followed by affirming their preparedness and ability, such as saying to themselves, "I am ready, and I can do this." This kind of ritual can significantly enhance focus, providing a familiar structure that helps calm nerves and triggers a mental state conducive to peak performance.

Lastly, integrating focus drills into daily training routines can significantly enhance a gymnast's ability to concentrate. Simple exercises like balancing on one leg while solving a math problem or practicing routines with background distractions like music or conversation can train them to maintain focus regardless of external interruptions.

These drills improve their ability to concentrate during their gymnastics routines and enhance their overall cognitive flexibility, which can be beneficial in academic settings as well. By incorporating these techniques into their training, young gymnasts can significantly improve their focus and concentration, key components that are as critical to their success in gymnastics as physical strength and agility.

Through mindfulness, creating a distraction-free environment, routine pre-performance rituals, and specific focus-enhancing drills, they can build the mental fortitude necessary to excel not just on the mat, but in all areas of life.

5.4 Handling Frustration and Setbacks

In the gymnastics arena, just as in life, not every day can be about triumphs and perfect landings. Young gymnasts sometimes face frustrations and setbacks despite their best efforts and preparations. So, it's crucial to understand where these feelings come from and how to manage them effectively.

Often, frustration in gymnastics arises from a mismatch between expectations and reality. This might be a young gymnast struggling to master a new skill as quickly as their peers, or facing repeated falls during practice. These moments can feel disheartening, but they're a natural part of the learning process.

The first step in managing frustration is recognizing its sources. This might involve a detailed discussion with your child about what is causing their distress. Is it a particular skill that's proving difficult, or is it the pressure of upcoming competitions?

Once identified, you can begin to address these issues directly. For example, if a skill is the problem, try splitting it into shorter or less demanding parts. If competition pressure is the issue, work on strategies to enhance mental resilience and focus.

Implementing structured breaks can be a highly effective strategy. Gymnastics, while rewarding, can be intensely demanding, and continuous practice without adequate rest can exacerbate feelings of frustration.

Insist on your child taking regular breaks, not only to rest their body but also to clear their mind. During these breaks, engaging in entirely different activities can provide mental refreshment, helping them return to practice with renewed energy and perspective.

Setting realistic expectations is another fundamental aspect of managing frustration. Young gymnasts must understand that progress in gymnastics is often slow and incremental. Celebrate small improvements to show them that progress isn't only about big wins; it's also about tiny steps forward.

Additionally, maintain open lines of communication with coaches (once your young gymnast has progressed to working with a coach) to ensure that their teaching methods and expectations align with your child's developmental stage. Coaches can provide priceless feedback that helps adjust goals and expectations to more realistic levels.

When setbacks do occur, framing them as learning opportunities can transform a potentially negative experience into a valuable lesson. Discuss what didn't go as planned and explore why that might have been. This process not only aids in problem-solving but also helps develop a more resilient mindset.

Encourage your child to come up with ideas on what they can try differently next time. Involving them in the solution process empowers them and helps alleviate feelings of helplessness that often accompany setbacks.

Building a Strong Support System

A robust support system is a cornerstone of any athlete's success, particularly in a sport as challenging as gymnastics. This system should include coaches, family members, and peers, each playing a unique role in the gymnast's development.

Coaches provide professional guidance, skill improvement strategies, and motivational support. Family members offer emotional support, understanding, and encouragement, while peers can relate to the gymnastic journey, share experiences, and offer camaraderie.

Create an environment where open communication is encouraged and emotions can be freely expressed. This could be through regular family meetings where each member shares their challenges and successes or setting aside time after practice for your child to talk about their day with you. When young gymnasts feel heard and understood, their emotional burden is significantly reduced.

Additionally, prompt your child to build friendships with their gymnastics peers. These relationships can be a source of support and motivation, as they understand the unique challenges of the sport. Peer support can also foster a healthy competitive spirit that can motivate your child to push their boundaries in a constructive environment.

By proactively managing frustration and setbacks through understanding their sources, implementing strategic breaks, setting realistic expectations, learning from setbacks, and nurturing a strong support network, young gymnasts can navigate the ups and downs of their training with resilience and grace.

These strategies help maintain their passion for the sport and equip them with skills to handle life's challenges, making them stronger both on and off the gymnastics floor.

5.5 The Importance of Persistence in Gymnastics

Persistence is the fuel that drives us as humans toward reaching our peaks, no matter how steep the climb. A gymnast's journey is dotted with challenges that test their resilience, pushing them to learn not just how to perform spectacular flips but also how to bounce back with more strength after a fall.

To build this resilience, your child must develop a mindset that views challenges as catalysts for growth rather than roadblocks. One effective way to do this is through structured challenge settings. This involves creating scenarios slightly beyond their current capabilities, encouraging them to leave their comfort zone.

For instance, if a gymnast has mastered a basic handstand, the next challenge could be to hold it for longer or to perform it on a different surface. These challenges should be designed to be achievable but demanding, promoting a gradual build-up of confidence and skill. Regularly overcoming these challenges instills a belief in their ability to tackle and conquer difficulties, which is the essence of resilience.

The stories of well-known gymnasts who have demonstrated exceptional persistence can also serve as powerful motivators. Share real stories about gymnasts who returned to compete in the Olympics after career-threatening injuries or other setbacks. Such stories highlight the determination and grit required to overcome significant adversity.

Discussing these examples can inspire young gymnasts, showing them that persistence can lead to remarkable achievements. They learn that setbacks are not the end of the road but opportunities to grow stronger and more determined.

Rewarding effort over results plays a critical role in encouraging persistence. In gymnastics, where perfectionism can often take hold, it's important to shift the focus from flawless execution to consistent effort.

Acknowledging the hard work your child puts into training, regardless of the outcome, reinforces the value of persistence. It teaches them that effort is more important than occasional victories, setting them up for a long-term commitment to improvement.

For instance, instead of praising only when they win a medal, celebrate the extra hours they put in at the gym or their decision to practice even when they weren't feeling up to it.

Dealing with plateaus—periods where no visible progress seems to be made—can be particularly frustrating for young gymnasts. During such times, it's helpful to revisit and possibly readjust their goals. Sometimes, setting smaller, more immediate objectives can reignite momentum.

Introducing new activities or cross-training can also provide a fresh perspective and rekindle enthusiasm. For example, incorporating dance or swimming into their routine can improve their gymnastics skills from different angles, making the process more engaging. It's also beneficial to remind them that progress doesn't always happen in a straight line and that plateaus can be a sign of impending breakthroughs, encouraging them to stay the course and keep pushing.

Through these strategies, persistence becomes woven into the fabric of their gymnastics practice, transforming their approach to challenges and setbacks. It teaches them that every fall has a lesson and that every effort brings them one step closer to their goals.

This relentless pursuit of growth, powered by persistence, shapes them into better gymnasts and more resilient individuals ready to leap over life's hurdles with grace and strength.

5.6 Celebrating Small Victories: Motivation Boosters

In gymnastics, where challenges loom large, and the pressure to perform can be overwhelming, recognizing and celebrating every small victory can be a powerful motivator. These moments of triumph, whether perfecting a stance that was once wobbly or finally nailing a routine that took weeks to learn, are crucial.

They serve as reminders of progress and fuel the journey forward. Embracing these achievements can significantly boost a young gymnast's motivation and self-esteem, transforming their training environment into a space of encouragement and positive reinforcement.

The power of positive reinforcement in shaping behavior and encouraging persistence is well-documented. In gymnastics, this means celebrating the achievements and the effort put into each practice session.

One effective way to do this is through a structured reward system. This doesn't have to be elaborate; it can be as simple as a chart on the fridge where stickers are added for each small achievement. After a certain number of stickers, a small reward can be given.

This method makes the progress visible and tangible, providing continuous motivation. Rewards should ideally be linked to effort and personal achievements, rather than comparing with others, to foster a healthy sense of self-improvement.

Involving peers and family in the celebration of these achievements can magnify their impact. When a gymnast's support network acknowledges their successes, it reinforces their sense of accomplishment and belonging.

Organizing small 'celebration meets' where gymnasts can showcase their skills to family and friends can be an excellent way to do this. Here, each child gets a moment in the spotlight to demonstrate their improvements, followed by collective applause and recognition.

This boosts their confidence and strengthens the social bonds within their support network, creating a community that thrives on mutual encouragement and appreciation.

Nudging young gymnasts to keep a success journal can also be invaluable. In this journal, they can record their achievements and how they felt about them and reflect on the steps that led to those successes.

This practice helps them internalize what they learned, making it easier to replicate that success in the future. It also serves as a personal record of their journey, which they can look back on during tougher times for motivation.

Prompt them to write about how they overcame challenges or improved on something they struggled with, turning the journal into a repository of personal growth and resilience. Focusing on these small yet significant victories helps shape a gymnast's mindset to appreciate every step forward, no matter how small.

This approach enhances their current gymnastic endeavors and instills a lifelong appreciation for growth and learning. It teaches them to see value in the process itself, not just the outcome, breeding a positive attitude that transcends sports and affects all areas of life.

Final Thoughts

This chapter has explored the crucial mental aspects of gymnastics that support young athletes in their training and competitions. These insights are designed to fortify their mental resilience, from setting strategic goals and managing fears to enhancing focus and handling frustrations.

We've also emphasized the importance of celebrating each achievement, which fuels further effort and perseverance. As we close this chapter, we will begin digging deeper into another critical component of gymnastics: preventing injuries.

SIX

Safety First: Preventing Injuries

T he journey might be emotionally complex for every parent facing a sport with inherent danger. You watch as your child, filled with enthusiasm, is practicing a new gymnastics routine in your backyard. As you see them pivot and leap, a mix of pride and concern crosses your mind. You're thrilled to see their progress, but you're also aware of the risks involved in such a physically demanding activity.

Gymnastics, while an excellent sport for physical fitness and confidence-building, comes with its share of injury risks, from minor bruises to more severe sprains and fractures. Understanding and mitigating these risks is crucial for keeping your young gymnast safe and healthy.

6.1 Common Gymnastics Injuries and How to Avoid Them

The most frequent injuries in gymnastics include sprains, strains, and fractures. Sprains often occur in the wrists and ankles and result from overuse or landing improperly after a jump or flip.

Strains, however, are more about the muscles—think of a pulled muscle from stretching too far or without proper warm-up.

Fractures can occur from falls or repeated stress on bones, particularly in younger gymnasts whose bones are still developing. The mechanics of these injuries usually involve either acute trauma from a fall or stress from repetitive movements.

Preventive Measures

The key to preventing these injuries lies in a combination of proper warm-up routines, correct technique, and protective gear. Encouraging your child to thoroughly warm up before starting practice is non-negotiable.

A good warm-up increases blood flow to the muscles, making them more flexible and less prone to injuries. Dynamic stretches, which involve moving parts of the body gradually increasing reach and speed of movement, are particularly beneficial before gymnastics routines.

Teaching correct techniques is another critical preventive measure. Incorrect form not only hampers performance but also dramatically increases injury risk. For instance, landing with knees straight can put undue stress on the joints, leading to potential injuries.

Here, the role of a knowledgeable coach or instructor becomes indispensable. Even if formal gymnastics classes aren't an option right now, many professionals offer virtual sessions or can provide feedback on videos of your child's practice.

Protective gear such as wrist supports, knee pads, and proper footwear can also play a significant role in injury prevention. These items provide support and cushioning, reducing the impact on joints and muscles during high-risk movements.

Investing in a high-quality gymnastics mat for home practice is also wise, as it provides the necessary cushioning and support needed to safely practice routines.

Environmental Safety Tips

We've covered some of this in past chapters, but it bears repeating. Creating a safe practice environment at home is just as important as teaching proper technique and using the right gear. Ensure the practice area is spacious enough for gymnastics activities—free from obstacles like furniture and hard surfaces.

The flooring should be even and adequately padded. If you use gymnastics apparatus like beams or bars, make sure they are stable and well-maintained. Regular checks for wear and tear can prevent accidents caused by equipment failure.

Educational Resources

Numerous resources are available for parents and young gymnasts eager to deepen their understanding of injury prevention. Websites like USA Gymnastics offer a wealth of information on safe practice guidelines and injury prevention tips.

Books and online courses on sports safety can also be helpful. They provide detailed insights into how injuries occur and how to prevent them through proper technique and environmental management.

Incorporating the strategies you learn into your child's gymnastics practice minimizes the risk of injury and promotes a healthier and more enjoyable sporting experience.

As they flip, twist, and leap, you'll have peace of mind knowing you've taken proactive steps to keep them safe, letting them focus on the joy and challenge of gymnastics.

6.2 First Aid Basics for Gymnastics Injuries

While we've discussed minimizing risks, it's equally important to be prepared should injuries occur. A well-stocked first aid kit is your first line of defense, providing the tools you need to address common injuries quickly and effectively.

In your gymnastics-specific first aid kit, you should include items like adhesive bandages of various sizes, sterile gauze pads, adhesive tape, and scissors. These are paramount for covering and protecting minor cuts and abrasions. Elastic bandages and cold packs are necessary for treating sprains and strains, helping reduce swelling and temporarily immobilize the affected area.

Antiseptic wipes or sprays are essential for cleaning wounds, and topical creams or ointments can soothe scrapes or mild burns. Finally, remember to include a list of emergency contacts, including your family doctor and local emergency services, along with any known allergies or medical conditions your child may have, so you have this on hand should a need arise.

Next, take time to understand how to handle common gymnastic injuries like cuts, bruises, and sprains. For minor cuts and abrasions, the first step is always to clean the area gently but thoroughly to prevent infection. Use antiseptic wipes or rinse the wound under clean water. Applying a thin layer of antibiotic ointment before covering the cut with a sterile bandage can also help promote healing.

Bruises, although often minor, can still be painful. Applying a cold pack to the bruised area in intervals of about 15 minutes can help reduce swelling and numb the pain.

If your child experiences a sprain, remember the RICE method: Rest, Ice, Compression, and Elevation. Have them rest the injured limb, apply an ice pack wrapped in a cloth to avoid ice burn, use an elastic bandage to compress the area gently, and keep the limb elevated above the heart to reduce swelling.

The role of non-medical treatment like the RICE method can't be overstated in the initial treatment of minor injuries. Rest prevents further strain on the injured area, reducing the risk of worsening the injury. Ice helps reduce swelling and numb the area, which can alleviate pain.

Compression helps to minimize swelling, and elevation also aids in this process by decreasing blood flow to the area, which can help reduce inflammation and pain. These steps, while simple, are incredibly effective in managing minor injuries until they can heal or until professional medical advice can be sought if needed.

Lastly, it's beneficial for both parents and coaches to have basic first aid training. Knowledge of how to properly respond to injuries can significantly affect the management and outcome of common gymnastics injuries.

First aid courses are widely available through organizations like the Red Cross or local community centers. These courses teach the practical skills needed to treat injuries and how to assess a situation quickly and effectively, ensuring that your young gymnast receives the best care possible in the event of an accident.

Being prepared with the right knowledge and tools will give you peace of mind and ensure that you are ready to support your child and keep their gymnastics experience as safe and enjoyable as possible.

6.3 When to See a Doctor: Recognizing Serious Injuries

As a parent, sometimes the hardest part isn't just watching your child fall, but knowing when a tumble requires more than just a comforting hug and an ice pack. While many minor injuries can be treated at home, there are times when you should seek professional medical attention.

Understanding the signs of serious injuries like suspected broken bones or concussions can be the key to preventing long-term damage and ensuring a safe return to gymnastics for your child.

For instance, if your child has taken a fall and now can't put weight on a limb, or if there's visible deformity like a wrist looking out of place, these are clear signs of possible fractures.

Similarly, if your child appears dazed after a head impact, repeatedly asks the same questions, or has trouble recalling events before the fall, these could be signs of a concussion. Other red flags include severe pain that doesn't improve with rest, swelling that quickly worsens, or any joint that appears abnormally bent or positioned.

Also, watch for signs of shock, such as pale, cold, clammy skin, rapid breathing, or a weak and rapid pulse. These symptoms demand immediate medical attention.

The importance of not delaying medical consultation can't be overstated. For bone fractures, swift treatment can prevent complications like misaligned healing, which might later require surgical intervention. In the case of concussions, early diagnosis and management are crucial to prevent further injury and facilitate a safe recovery.

Delays can extend recovery periods and potentially lead to more severe consequences. Therefore, if you suspect a serious injury, it's better to err on the side of caution and get your child evaluated by a healthcare professional promptly.

Navigating an emergency medical visit can be stressful, but knowing what to expect can help you manage the situation more effectively. When you arrive at the hospital or urgent care, be prepared to provide detailed information about how the injury occurred and your child's medical history. This includes any previous injuries, current medications, and known allergies.

During the evaluation, your child might undergo physical exams and imaging tests like X-rays or MRIs to determine the extent of the injury. Being familiar with these procedures and explaining them to your child beforehand can help alleviate some of their anxiety.

Follow-up care is also crucial for serious injuries. This might involve additional visits to a specialist, such as an orthopedist for fractures or a neurologist for concussions. These specialists can provide more detailed assessments and tailored treatment plans.

Rehabilitation, including physical therapy or specific exercises, often plays a key role in recovery. Adhering to the prescribed rehabilitation plan and keeping all follow-up appointments are essential to ensure your child heals properly and regains full function. Additionally, gradual re-introduction to gymnastics should be closely monitored by healthcare professionals to prevent the recurrence of injury.

Understanding when to seek medical help and how to navigate the care process ensures that your child receives the necessary treatment to return to their beloved sport safely. It also teaches them to listen to their bodies and speak up about their pain, fostering a healthier approach to sports and physical activity.

By recognizing the signs of serious injuries and acting promptly, you not only safeguard your child's physical health but also their long-term well-being and success in gymnastics.

6.4 Safe Practice Habits: Dos and Don'ts

When nurturing a young gymnast's passion at home, creating a safe and supportive environment is as important as the physical space where they practice. Regularly checking the practice area to ensure it is free from hazards is a good starting point.

This might seem straightforward, but it goes beyond just tidying up. It involves examining the area for any potential risks such as slippery surfaces, sharp corners, or unstable equipment. For example, before each session, take a few moments to scan the room or backyard.

Make sure that the floor is clear of objects that could cause trips or falls, and check that all equipment is secure and in good condition. If you're using items like weights or resistance bands, store them safely away when not in use to prevent accidents.

Being sure to supervise practices is very important, especially for younger children or when a gymnast is trying out new skills. Supervision means more than just being present; it involves active engagement with what your child is doing. This doesn't necessarily require technical knowledge of gymnastics. It's about being there to offer encouragement, ensure they follow safety protocols, and intervene if you notice any unsafe practices.

For instance, if your child is working on a new jump or flip, be close enough to assist or catch them if they lose balance. Your presence can also comfort them, as they know they have your support as they challenge themselves with new moves.

Communicating safety rules effectively helps confirm the rules are followed. This starts with clear explanations of what is expected and why it matters. For younger gymnasts, use simple language and concrete examples to explain how following the rules helps them avoid injuries. You might say, "We keep our toys away from the practice mat so we don't trip on them and fall."

Regular reminders and practicing what you preach—by following safety protocols yourself—reinforce these messages. Also, consider creating a visual reminder like a poster with safety rules illustrated on it, which can be a fun project to do together. Place it where your child can easily see it during practice, serving as a constant reminder in a friendly, non-intrusive way.

Cultivating a culture of safety in your home gymnastics setup involves prioritizing well-being over performance. It's easy to get caught up in the excitement of perfecting a new move or routine, but safety should always come first. This means recognizing when to take a break if your child is tired, as fatigue can lead to sloppy execution and injuries.

It also means not pushing them to perform moves they're not ready for, physically or emotionally. Encourage a mindset where taking necessary precautions and speaking up about discomfort or fear isn't seen as a setback but as a smart approach to gymnastics. This applies to physical safety and emotional well-being, ensuring that your child feels confident and secure in their gymnastics journey.

By integrating these practices into your routine, you help create a safe and nurturing environment where your child can thrive as a gymnast and a confident and responsible individual.

Regular checks, active supervision, clear communication, and a culture that values safety over results are the pillars that support a robust and safe gymnastics practice at home.

6.5 Using Spotters: The Importance of Assistance

When your child is flipping through the air or balancing precariously on a beam, the presence of a spotter can be incredibly reassuring. A spotter plays a critical role in gymnastics, especially when athletes learn new skills or refine existing ones. Their primary responsibility is to ensure the gymnast's safety, helping prevent injuries by providing physical support during difficult maneuvers.

Think of spotters as guardians and facilitators in the gymnastics environment; they stand ready to intervene if a move goes awry, but they also provide the psychological comfort that allows gymnasts to attempt skills they might otherwise be too fearful to try.

The effectiveness of a spotter largely depends on their ability to perform their role correctly, which requires proper training and a deep understanding of gymnastic movements. Training for spotters should include learning the techniques needed to safely support different gymnastics skills.

This training is often provided in gymnastics clubs, but for parents or siblings acting as spotters at home, it's essential to seek guidance from resources that can offer it. Many online platforms provide video tutorials and detailed instructions on spotting techniques.

These resources often demonstrate the hand placements, body positioning, and timing required to spot various gymnastics moves, such as handstands, somersaults, and backflips. Understanding the correct spotting techniques is vital.

For instance, when spotting a handstand, the spotter should stand close to the gymnast, with one hand ready to support the gymnast's back and the other hand near the legs. This positioning allows the spotter to quickly provide support if the gymnast begins to fall, either by steadying them or by guiding them safely to the floor.

For more dynamic moves like flips or vaults, spotters must be vigilant, ready to adjust their support based on the gymnast's motion. This might involve supporting the gymnast's hips to help control their rotation or assisting with a safe landing by guiding their descent.

The psychological benefits of having a reliable spotter are also significant. When gymnasts feel secure in knowing that a competent spotter is present, their confidence increases. This security allows them to attempt and master skills that might otherwise seem too daunting.

The assurance of safety fosters a more adventurous and positive approach to learning, which is essential for progress in gymnastics. Particularly for children, who may feel nervous about performing certain moves, knowing someone is there to catch them can make all the difference in their willingness to engage and push their limits. This safety net protects them physically and builds their mental and emotional resilience, key components in the journey of any young athlete.

In essence, the role of a spotter is integral to the practice of gymnastics, especially in the developmental stages of a young gymnast's training. Their presence can prevent physical injuries and elevate a gymnast's confidence, empowering them to reach new heights in their skills.

For parents and coaches, investing time in learning effective spotting techniques and understanding the nuances of this role can dramatically enhance the safety and quality of a gymnast's training experience. As your child spins, jumps, and soars, a knowledgeable, attentive spotter makes sure their gymnastics experience is as safe as it is exhilarating, allowing them to fully embrace the challenges and joys of the sport.

6.6 Equipment Safety Checks: Keeping Gear in Good Condition

Verifying the safety and longevity of gymnastics equipment is not just about making a purchase and using it; it involves regular maintenance and keen observation. Establishing a routine maintenance schedule is crucial. Think of it like caring for a car—regular check-ups keep it running smoothly and prevent issues down the line.

For gymnastics equipment, a monthly inspection is a good baseline. During these checks, tighten any loose bolts or screws on apparatus like bars or beams. Check mats for any tears or flattening of padding, which can reduce their effectiveness in cushioning falls. Additionally, inspect any attachments or supports for stability and wear.

Identifying wear and tear early can prevent accidents caused by equipment failure. For instance, look for fraying or signs of excessive wear on items like gymnastic rings or ropes. For beams and bars, check for cracks or splits in the material. These can often be felt as much as seen, so running a hand over surfaces during inspections can help detect issues that aren't immediately visible.

The presence of rust on metal parts can weaken the equipment, making it unsafe, so keep an eye out for any signs of oxidation, especially if your equipment is stored in damp or humid conditions.

Proper storage of gymnastics equipment also plays a significant role in its maintenance. Mats should be stored flat or rolled up, not folded, which can cause creases that compromise their structural integrity. Apparatus like beams, bars, or pommel horses should be stored in a clean, dry area to prevent moisture damage.

It's also wise to cover equipment when not in use to protect it from dust and other environmental factors. If space allows, dedicated storage areas with appropriate racks or shelving can keep your gear organized and in good condition, making it easy to check each piece when it's time for maintenance.

Finally, there comes a point when upgrading or replacing equipment is necessary to maintain safety standards. Regular maintenance can extend the life of your equipment, but all gymnastics gear has a lifespan. Upgrading equipment is essential when wear and tear become too significant to repair or when advances in safety technology offer superior options.

For instance, newer models of mats or padding might provide better shock absorption due to advancements in materials. Furthermore, if your child's skill level has outgrown the current equipment—like moving from a low balance beam to a high beam—it's time to upgrade to match their development and keep them safe.

Keeping gymnastics equipment in good condition is a must for the safety and effectiveness of every practice session. Regular checks and maintenance, understanding when to upgrade, and knowing how to properly store equipment can significantly extend its life and ensure it safely supports your child's gymnastics activities. Integrating these practices creates a secure environment that lets your young gymnast explore and excel without unnecessary risks.

Moving forward, we'll delve into the exciting world of advanced gymnastics and uncover stories of inspiration that are sure to be a source of motivatation for your child.

SEVEN

Inspirational Stories from the Gymnastics World

As a young child, flipping through the pages of a gymnastics history book can be utterly awe-inspiring. They see tales of young gymnasts who, not much older than themselves, leaped beyond the ordinary to carve their names into the annals of gymnastics history. For any young gymnast or a parent supporting their child's gymnastic dreams, these stories are not just entertaining; they fuel their aspirations.

In this chapter, we delve into the lives of such remarkable young athletes who have made significant impacts in gymnastics before even reaching adulthood. Their early starts, the challenges they navigated, and the heights they soared to serve as powerful motivation for anyone at this sport's threshold.

7.1 Profiles of Young Gymnasts Who Made History

Historic Achievements

Throughout the history of gymnastics, several young prodigies have emerged, transforming their youthful zeal into spectacular performances that have left indelible marks on the sport.

Take, for instance, Nadia Comaneci, the Romanian gymnast who, at just 14 years old, scored the first perfect 10.0 at the Olympic Games. Her achievement at the 1976 Montreal Olympics wasn't just a personal victory; it redefined what was possible in gymnastics, pushing the boundaries and setting a new pinnacle of excellence.

Then there's Simone Biles, who became the most decorated American gymnast at a young age, dazzling the world with her incredible power and artistry. These athletes, through their groundbreaking performances, have not only collected medals but also inspired countless young gymnasts around the globe to dream big and push harder.

Early Beginnings

The journey to greatness often begins early, especially in gymnastics, where early training can make a profound difference. Most gymnastic prodigies start training as toddlers, learning to channel their boundless energy into disciplined forms and movements.

For instance, Shawn Johnson began gymnastics at three years old, driven by a natural inclination for tumbling and flipping that was evident even in her early childhood.

These stories highlight the importance of nurturing an intrinsic passion from a young age, providing the right support and resources, and the role parents and coaches play in recognizing and fostering potential from the outset.

Training Regimens

The road to success in gymnastics is paved with relentless training, resilience, and an unwavering commitment to excellence. Young gymnasts often undergo rigorous training schedules that involve multiple hours of practice each day, supplemented by strength training, flexibility sessions, and mental conditioning.

The intensity of these regimens is captured in the words of Gabby Douglas, who once said, "Hard days are the best because that's when champions are made." This statement reflects the rigorous nature of gymnastic training and the sheer perseverance required to excel.

The discipline instilled through such training extends beyond the gym. It influences gymnasts' approach to life and challenges, shaping them into individuals who strive for excellence in every endeavor.

Even More Inspiration

Olga Korbut, known for her emotional performances and daring skills, once remarked, "I taught [the world] that emotion and gymnastics go together." Her words remind us that gymnastics, like any other form of art, is not just about physical prowess but also about expressing oneself.

These words are powerful, reinforcing the idea that every young gymnast can make the sport their own. Such a quote can be a motivational mantra, too, encouraging gymnasts to blend passion with practice as they carve their own paths in the gymnastics world.

As we explore these stories, they do more than narrate the past; they ignite the possibilities of what can be achieved with dedication and passion. For every young gymnast practicing in a home gym or dreaming big dreams, these stories are a testament to where passion, discipline, and the support of loved ones can lead.

They guide young athletes as they flip, twist, and leap toward their gymnastics goals, reminding them that they, too, can leave a mark on this sport. In these tales of young gymnasts who reshaped the landscape of gymnastics, we find inspiration and the blueprint for nurturing the champions of tomorrow.

7.2 Stories of Perseverance: Gymnasts Who Overcame Adversity

Overcoming Injuries

The journey of a gymnast is rarely without its hurdles, particularly when it comes to injuries. Consider the story of a particular gymnast who, at the peak of her career, faced a potentially career-ending injury. During a routine practice, she suffered a severe knee injury, tearing her ACL. The road to recovery was long and fraught with doubt. Yet, instead of succumbing to despair, she channeled her energies into a rigorous rehabilitation program.

Her days were filled with physical therapy, strength training, and mental conditioning. Each small step in her rehab was a victory, a testament to her unwavering spirit. After months of hard work, not only did she return to the sport, but she also went on to win national titles. Her story is a powerful reminder of the resilience human beings can demonstrate.

It teaches young gymnasts that injuries and setbacks are not the end of their dreams but merely obstacles that can be overcome with perseverance and a positive mindset.

Dealing with Personal Challenges

Beyond the physical challenges, many gymnasts navigate personal hardships that test their resolve. Take the example of a young gymnast who grew up in a financially disadvantaged family.

The cost of training, equipment, and competitions was a constant burden. Yet, her passion for gymnastics drove her to seek creative solutions. She took on part-time jobs, applied for scholarships, and participated in community fundraisers. Her community rallied around her, inspired by her dedication and passion.

This gymnast's journey underscores the importance of community support and the power of determination. It shows young athletes that their circumstances do not define their potential and that with resourcefulness and support, barriers can be transformed into stepping stones.

Mental Toughness

The mental challenges in gymnastics are as demanding as the physical ones. Many gymnasts struggle with fear, anxiety, and self-doubt. Consider a gymnast who, despite her talent, struggled with performance anxiety. The pressure of competition would overwhelm her, affecting her performance.

Recognizing this, she began working with a sports psychologist, learning techniques to manage her anxiety. She practiced visualization, imagining herself performing perfectly before each event. Gradually, her confidence grew, and her competition results improved. Her story highlights the critical role mental health plays in sports.

It teaches young gymnasts the importance of mental resilience and the effectiveness of seeking help when needed. It also illustrates that overcoming psychological hurdles often leads to improved performance and personal growth.

Role Models

These stories of perseverance show young gymnasts that, like their heroes, they, too, can overcome adversity. They teach lessons in resilience, hard work, and the importance of mental toughness. Each story shows the human spirit's capacity to overcome and the transformative power of gymnastics in shaping strong, resilient individuals.

As role models, these and other gymnasts exemplify the values of perseverance and courage, showing young athletes everywhere that with determination, support, and hard work, any obstacle can be overcome, and any dream can be achieved. They remind us that the true value of sports lies not just in medals and accolades but in the life lessons they teach and the character they build.

7.3 The Road to the Olympics: Inspirational Journeys

For many young gymnasts, the Olympics represent the pinnacle of achievement, a stage where years of dedication, sacrifices, and dreams converge. The path to the Olympics is a culmination of countless hours of training, overcoming personal and physical challenges, and the unwavering support of families and coaches.

From local meets to the grand international stages, each step is a building block in preparing a gymnast for the competitions and the intense scrutiny and pressure that comes with the Olympic Games.

The journey often begins in small, local gyms where young gymnasts learn the ropes of competitive gymnastics. Participating in these local competitions provides:

- Crucial early exposure to the competitive environment.
- Teaching young athletes about sportsmanship and discipline.
- The importance of routine execution under pressure.

As we progress through different levels, the competitions grow and the stakes increase. Regional and national championships are where Olympic hopefuls start to make their mark, attracting attention from national committees and sponsors. It's here that their potential for international competition is often first seriously considered.

For those who reach the level where they can contend for Olympic selection, the preparation intensifies. Training camps become a second home where gymnasts undergo rigorous routines to refine every movement to perfection. These camps are not just about physical training; they include comprehensive mental conditioning to prepare athletes for the psychological demands of performing on the world's biggest stage.

Sports psychologists work closely with gymnasts to enhance their mental resilience, teaching them techniques to manage stress, visualize success, and maintain focus amid the distractions of a global audience.

Nutrition also plays a critical role in an Olympic gymnast's preparation. Dietitians are part of the support team, ensuring that athletes receive the optimal balance of nutrients to fuel their intense training while maintaining peak physical condition.

The diet includes carefully planned meals rich in energy, lean proteins for muscle repair and recovery, and ample hydration to sustain long training sessions. This level of detailed nutritional planning is crucial in a sport where every ounce of energy counts and where athletes must maintain a specific weight and muscle mass to perform complex routines.

The Olympic experience itself is transformative. For gymnasts who reach this stage, it's a mix of nerve-wracking competition and exhilarating moments. Competing against the world's best, these athletes perform routines that they have practiced thousands of times, yet each performance is unique due to the intense pressure and high stakes.

The Olympic Village, the camaraderie with athletes from various sports and countries, and the global spotlight contribute to a life-changing experience that remains with them forever.

Life After the Olympics

Post-Olympics, gymnasts often face a new set of challenges and opportunities. While some continue competing, others retire, turning their focus to new careers within or outside the sport.

Transitioning to coaching is a common path, allowing former gymnasts to pass on their knowledge and experiences to the next generation. Coaching can be incredibly rewarding, as it offers a chance to shape young gymnasts' careers and stay connected to the sport they love.

Advocacy and mentorship are other avenues that retired gymnasts often pursue. Using their platform and experience, they advocate for the sport's development, work on initiatives to make gymnastics more accessible, and mentor young athletes navigating the complexities of competitive sports. Their insights are invaluable in shaping policies and programs that support the growth and well-being of gymnasts globally.

Furthermore, many gymnasts leverage their Olympic fame to embark on careers in media, business, or public speaking. Their stories of perseverance, peak performance, and overcoming adversity resonate widely, making them inspirational figures in various fields. Whether it's running a gymnastics-related business, engaging in motivational speaking, or participating in television and media projects, these athletes continue to inspire and influence long after their Olympic routines are done.

Navigating life after the Olympics involves adapting to new roles and finding new passions, but the discipline, resilience, and dedication honed during their gymnastics careers provide a strong foundation for success in any field. For these athletes, the end of their Olympic journey marks the beginning of new adventures, where they continue to inspire, lead, and make a difference.

7.4 Lessons from Professional Coaches

In the dynamic and demanding world of gymnastics, the role of a coach extends far beyond teaching techniques and routines. Renowned gymnastics coaches often share a common philosophy that focuses on developing the athlete as a whole, recognizing that each gymnast brings a unique set of skills, challenges, and aspirations to the mat.

These coaches emphasize the importance of fostering a positive, supportive environment while pushing gymnasts to reach their full potential. Their approach is holistic, prioritizing mental and emotional growth alongside physical training, because they understand that confidence and resilience are just as important as physical strength and agility.

One fundamental aspect of their coaching philosophy is the belief in the transformative power of gymnastics to build life skills. Coaches often talk about the sport as a platform for teaching discipline, dedication, and the value of hard work. They aim to instill these qualities in their gymnasts, preparing them for competition and life's many challenges.

This holistic approach is encapsulated in the words of a coach who once said, "Gymnastics is not just about winning medals. It's about setting goals, working hard to reach them, and learning from the journey." Such statements highlight how coaches use the sport as a tool for character building, emphasizing perseverance, teamwork, and personal integrity.

As we've covered, building a champion in gymnastics involves more than just physical training; it requires nurturing the athlete's mental and emotional strength. Coaches use various techniques to build confidence in young gymnasts. These include setting manageable goals that provide frequent opportunities for success, offering consistent and constructive feedback, and teaching athletes how to visualize successful performances.

Furthermore, coaches spend considerable time developing strong relationships with their gymnasts based on trust and mutual respect, which is crucial for mental and emotional development. They create a safe space where gymnasts feel valued and supported, encouraging them to take risks and push their boundaries without fear of judgment.

The coaching profession, however, has its challenges. One of the most common hurdles coaches face is balancing the need to push athletes to their limits with the need to ensure their physical and emotional well-being. This balancing act requires deeply understanding each gymnast's physical and psychological capabilities.

Coaches must recognize the signs of burnout and fatigue and know when to pull back or push forward. Another significant challenge is dealing with a team of gymnasts' diverse needs and personalities. Each athlete responds differently to training techniques, motivational strategies, and feedback. Coaches must constantly adapt their approaches to meet these varying needs, which requires a flexible, patient, and empathetic coaching style.

For parents and novice coaches guiding young gymnasts, advice from experienced coaches can be invaluable. These experts emphasize the importance of focusing on the process rather than the outcome. Celebrating small achievements and consistent effort helps young gymnasts develop a love for the sport and a motivation to improve, independent of competition results.

Experienced coaches also stress the importance of communication—listening to the athletes' feedback, understanding their goals, and adjusting training plans accordingly. Additionally, they recommend educating oneself continuously about the latest gymnastics techniques, safety protocols, and psychological training methods to provide the best guidance possible.

Hopefully, with these insights and techniques from seasoned coaches, parents and novice coaches will be equipped with the tools they need to support their young gymnasts effectively. The lessons learned from these coaching philosophies and practices enhance the training environment and ensure that the gymnasts' journey in the sport is as rewarding and enriching as possible.

7.5 How Failures Lead to Success in Gymnastics

In gymnastics, where precision and perfection often take the spotlight, it's the unseen hours of failed attempts and not-quite-there moments that truly shape a gymnast's career.

It's important to remember that every failed attempt is a step towards mastery, and every misstep teaches resilience and adaptability. This understanding can transform the way young gymnasts perceive their own journeys, helping them embrace failures as milestones in their growth rather than setbacks.

One compelling narrative involves a gymnast who, despite being exceptionally talented, repeatedly failed to clinch the top spot at major competitions. Each loss was a blow to her confidence, yet it was these very experiences that became her greatest teachers. Through each failure, she learned to refine her techniques, enhance her routines, and, most importantly, toughen her mental game.

The turning point came when she failed to qualify for a prestigious international competition, a disappointment that led her to switch coaches and overhaul her training regimen. This change marked a drastic shift in her approach to gymnastics, focusing more on mental conditioning and consistency rather than just peak performance.

The result was not just a comeback but a spectacular win at the next world championships, proving that her failures were not in vain but were crucial steps towards her ultimate success.

The key lessons from such stories are manifold. First, they teach the importance of grit—the ability to persevere through setbacks and continue working toward one's goals. Grit isn't just about working hard; it's about maintaining passion and perseverance over the long term, especially when progress seems slow and victories are hard to come by.

Secondly, these stories highlight the importance of adaptability. Successful gymnasts learn to adapt their techniques, embrace new training methods, and sometimes even alter their goals based on the lessons learned from their failures. This adaptability ensures they continually evolve and improve, turning potential stumbling blocks into stepping stones.

Encouraging a growth mindset in young gymnasts is crucial for them to see the value in every failed attempt. A growth mindset, as opposed to a fixed mindset, thrives on challenge and sees failure not as evidence of unintelligence or lack of talent but as a heartening springboard for growth and for stretching our existing abilities.

This perspective encourages gymnasts to embrace challenges, persist despite setbacks, and see effort as a path to mastery. When young gymnasts learn to view their failures as necessary parts of learning, they are more likely to take on challenges and persevere through difficulties.

Teach your young gymnast that failure is not the opposite of success; it's part of success. Each misstep on the beam, each fall from the bars, and each stumble during a floor routine carries valuable lessons that are integral to a gymnast's growth and improvement.

By embracing these moments, learning from them, and using them to fuel their determination and refine their skills, they can turn their failures into a foundation for future success.

This approach builds stronger, more resilient athletes. It encourages them to approach life with the same courage and determination, viewing every challenge as an opportunity to learn, grow, and, ultimately, succeed.

7.6 Celebrating Diversity in Gymnastics

Gymnastics, much like any other global sport, presents a beautiful tapestry woven from diverse backgrounds, each bringing its unique thread to the overall picture. From small gymnasiums in remote areas to grand Olympic stages, the sport has seen an incredible variety of gymnasts from different countries, ethnicities, and socioeconomic backgrounds.

This diversity not only enriches the sport by introducing various skills and styles but also serves as a powerful reminder of the sport's universal appeal and accessibility. A young gymnast in a developing country, practicing on makeshift equipment, can aspire to the same heights as a gymnast from a well-equipped gym in a major city.

The stories of these gymnasts, who come from varied backgrounds and overcome numerous barriers to achieve greatness, are not just inspiring; they are instrumental in promoting a deeper understanding and appreciation of the sport's inclusive nature.

The history of gymnastics is replete with examples of gymnasts who have broken barriers, challenging the norms and paving the way for others. Consider the groundbreaking achievements of gymnasts who competed against their peers, societal expectations, and racial prejudices.

These athletes stood as pioneers, carving out spaces for themselves and future generations in a sport where they were once underrepresented. Their success stories show great resilience and determination, inspiring young gymnasts from similar backgrounds to pursue their dreams with renewed vigor and hope. These narratives are crucial, highlighting the sport's evolution towards greater inclusivity and equality.

Gymnastics has also seen a significant impact from various cultures worldwide, each contributing its unique flair and techniques. For instance, the elegance and precision often seen in Asian gymnasts' routines reflect their cultural emphasis on discipline and perfection, while the expressive and dynamic performances of Latin American gymnasts mirror their cultural vibrancy and passion.

This global influence is what makes gymnastics continually evolving and exciting. It's a sport that demands physical excellence and celebrates cultural expressions, allowing gymnasts to bring parts of their heritage to their performances, enriching the sport's diversity.

We can always do more to promote inclusivity in gymnastics. This should be more than just acknowledging the need for diversity; it involves active efforts to create environments where every gymnast feels welcomed, valued, and supported.

It's about gymnastics clubs, coaches, and associations going the extra mile to ensure that gymnastics training and competitions are accessible to everyone, regardless of their background. This could mean implementing programs that reach out to underrepresented communities, offering scholarships to talented gymnasts who might not otherwise afford training, or hosting inclusive events that celebrate diversity.

By fostering an inclusive culture, the gymnastics community can ensure that it champions diversity and thrives on it, reflecting the true spirit of sport — unity in diversity.

Celebrating diversity in gymnastics is not just about making the sport more inclusive; it's a powerful movement toward a global fraternity where every gymnast can aspire to be their best without barriers. It teaches young gymnasts the invaluable lessons of respect, equality, and unity, preparing them for competitions and life in a diverse world.

As gymnastics continues to evolve, it promises to become a beacon of diversity and inclusion, where we can all enjoy the sport's universal appeal and the shared human spirit that strives for excellence.

Wrapping Up

In this chapter, we've explored the vibrant world of gymnastics, celebrating athletes who've made history, defied the odds, and brought their unique cultural influences to the sport. Through their stories, we've seen how gymnastics is more than just a competitive sport; it's a global community that aims for inspiration and diversity.

These narratives inspire and challenge us to continue pushing for a more inclusive and equitable gymnastics environment. As we turn the page to the next chapter, we carry forward the spirit of unity and the celebration of diversity, aiming to make gymnastics accessible and enjoyable for everyone, everywhere.

EIGHT

Beyond Basics: Preparing for the Next Level

As you watch your child progress from where they started, you'll inevitably wonder: "Is it time for more structured gymnastics classes?" It's a thrilling and somewhat nerve-wracking question. Stepping up from practicing gymnastics at home to joining professional classes marks a significant milestone in your child's gymnastics adventure.

It's about more than just learning new flips and tricks; it's a journey that could shape their confidence, discipline, and passion for the sport. Let's navigate through the signs and considerations that will help you determine if your child is ready to take this exciting step forward.

8.1 Evaluating Readiness for Professional Gymnastics Classes

Assessing Skill Level

Determining whether your child is ready for professional gymnastics classes begins with an honest assessment of their current skills. This isn't just about how many tricks they can perform or how perfectly they execute a cartwheel. It's about understanding the depth of their foundational gymnastics knowledge, their mastery of basic techniques, and their readiness to learn more complex skills.

You can start by observing how well they maintain form and alignment during exercises, their understanding of gymnastics terminology, and their ability to perform routines with consistency.

Sometimes, having a checklist of key skills recommended for entry into professional classes can be beneficial, which you can often find through gymnastics websites or by consulting with a local gymnastics coach.

Physical Preparedness

Physical fitness is required in gymnastics, not only for performance but also for preventing injuries. Assessing your child's physical preparedness involves evaluating their strength, flexibility, endurance, and overall physical health. Are they able to handle the physical demands of longer, more frequent training sessions? Do they have the strength to safely attempt more advanced moves?

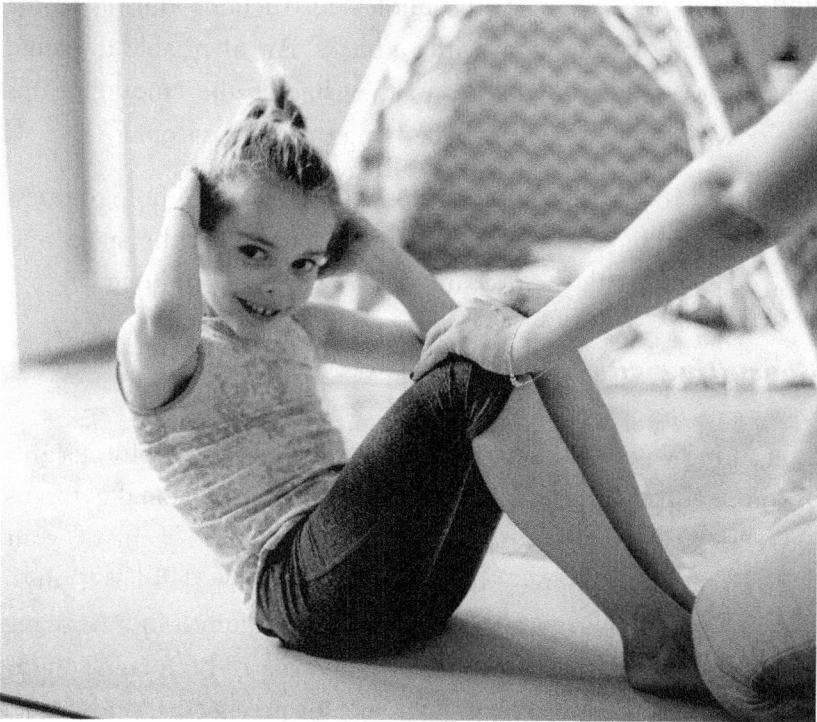

This assessment isn't about pushing your child to their physical limits; it's about ensuring they have a solid physical foundation to build upon. Regular fitness assessments, which can be as simple as noting improvements in how many push-ups or sit-ups they can do, or how long they can hold a balance, can give you a good indication of their physical readiness.

Emotional Maturity

Gymnastics is not just physically demanding; it's also mentally and emotionally challenging. The ability to handle structured environments, follow directions from coaches, and interact positively with peers are all indicators of emotional maturity.

Reflect on how your child handles instructions during home practice or how they deal with setbacks. Are they able to listen, learn, and apply feedback? Can they handle the emotional ups and downs that come with challenging training sessions?

Emotional readiness is just as important as physical preparedness because it influences how your child experiences the sport and how they cope with the pressures of more formal training.

Consulting with Professionals

Consulting with a professional coach can provide helpful insights if you're considering enrolling your child in professional gymnastics classes. A coach can offer an unbiased assessment of your child's readiness, taking into consideration their skill level, physical and emotional maturity, and even their interest in advancing in the sport. This consultation doesn't have to be formal; many gyms offer trial sessions or assessments for prospective students.

These sessions allow the coach to evaluate your child and give your child a taste of what professional gymnastics training would involve. It's a fantastic way for both of you to make an informed decision about taking this next step.

Interactive Element: Skills Assessment Checklist

Here's a simple checklist of skills and attributes to evaluate to help you and your child gauge readiness for professional gymnastics classes. Here's a recap of what you want to look for as you consider this exciting progression in your child's gymnastics journey.

- **Basic Skills Mastery**: Can your child perform foundational gymnastics moves with proper form and consistency?
- **Physical Fitness Level**: Does your child have the strength, flexibility, and endurance needed for more advanced training?
- **Emotional Readiness**: How well does your child handle instructions, feedback, and the emotional challenges of gymnastics?
- **Coach's Assessment**: Has a professional coach evaluated your child's readiness for more structured classes?

This checklist can be a practical starting point for your discussions with your child and any potential coaches, ensuring that the decision to move forward is thoughtful and well-informed. As you ponder these elements, remember that every child's development is unique.

Whether your child is ready now or needs a little more time, what matters most is their love for the sport and their enthusiasm for learning new skills. Each step forward, no matter how small, is a leap in their personal and athletic growth.

8.2 Choosing the Right Gymnastics Club: Factors to Consider

When the time comes to select a gymnastics club that fits your child's budding interest and growing skills, the process can feel as daunting as learning a new gymnastic routine itself. You want a place that teaches gymnastics and nurtures and supports your child's love for the sport.

A good gymnastics club can significantly influence your child's athletic development, so it's important to choose wisely. Here's how to sift through your options and find that perfect gymnastic home.

Reputation and Credentials

The reputation and credentials of a gymnastics club are fundamental to ensuring quality training and a positive experience. Start by researching the club's history and achievements. How long has it been established? What accolades or recognitions has the club received? Look for testimonials from other parents and reviews online to get a sense of other people's experiences.

It's also important to check the qualifications of the coaching staff. Are they certified through recognized gymnastics associations? What is their experience in coaching young gymnasts? A reputable club will transparently share their coaches' backgrounds, achievements, and coaching philosophies.

Attending a few competitions hosted by the club can also give you insights into how they operate and the level of their gymnasts' performances. This research will help you gauge whether the club's standards align with your expectations and if they can provide a conducive environment for your child's growth.

Facilities and Equipment

The quality of a gymnastics club's facilities and equipment plays a critical role in the safety and effectiveness of the training provided. Visit the club and take a tour of their facilities. Are the training areas well-maintained? Is the equipment modern and in good condition?

Check for safety measures like adequate matting, well-padded springs, and proper ventilation. Gyms that invest in high-quality equipment and maintain clean, safe facilities demonstrate a commitment to their gymnasts' welfare and professional development.

It's also worth noting how the space is organized. Is there enough room for all activities, or do the gymnasts seem cramped? A well-designed training space prevents injuries and creates an environment where gymnasts can focus on developing their skills without unnecessary distractions.

Programs Offered

When assessing a gymnastics club, consider the variety and appropriateness of their programs. Does the club provide programs that match your child's age and skill level? Are there advancement opportunities as your child progresses? The club needs to offer a structured progression of levels so that as your child grows in skill, they can continue to be challenged and engaged.

Additionally, ask about the flexibility of their programs. Some clubs offer more recreational paths, while others are geared toward competitive gymnastics. Depending on your child's interest and commitment level, the right program should offer the balance of fun and challenge that suits them best. Ask about the typical class sizes and the student-to-coach ratio to ensure your child will receive adequate attention and instruction.

Club Culture and Values

Finally, the club's culture and values should resonate with your family's values. A positive, supportive club culture is vital for fostering young gymnasts' confidence and love for the sport. Observe a few classes if possible, and note how coaches interact with gymnasts. Are they encouraging and supportive? How do they handle mistakes or setbacks?

Also, watch how the older or more advanced gymnasts behave; they often set the tone for the gym's environment. Are they supportive of each other, and do they seem happy and engaged?

A club that promotes healthy competition, mutual respect, and personal growth can have a profoundly positive impact on your child, both as an athlete and as an individual. Additionally, engaging with other parents can provide further insights into the club's community and whether it fits your family well.

Selecting the right gymnastics club is a significant decision that can influence your child's gymnastics experience profoundly. By carefully considering each of these factors, you can find a club that meets your child's developmental needs and supports their overall well-being and joy for the sport.

This careful deliberation ensures that the club you choose will be a place where your child can thrive, learn, and maybe one day, flip their way to greatness.

8.3 What to Expect in Your First Professional Lesson

When you and your child step into professional gymnastics classes for the first time, it can feel like entering a new universe where everyone else knows the rules except you. Understanding what a typical session entails helps demystify this new experience, setting you and your child up for a smoother transition.

Generally, a professional gymnastics lesson is structured to maximize learning and safety, typically starting with a warm-up session. This isn't just a few stretches; it's a comprehensive routine designed to prepare the body for the rigors of gymnastics. The warm-up might include cardiovascular exercises like jumping jacks or a short run, followed by dynamic stretching to limber up the muscles and joints.

After warming up, the main part of the lesson usually involves practicing specific gymnastics skills or routines. This could range from working on basic techniques like rolls and handstands for beginners, to more complex combinations and apparatus work for advanced students.

Coaches often use this time to introduce or refine new skills, providing hands-on guidance and corrections to ensure proper form and technique. This segment is highly interactive, with coaches continuously communicating what needs to be done and how to do it safely and effectively.

Toward the end of the class, there might be a cool-down period, which allows gymnasts to stretch out their muscles gently, helping to reduce soreness and prevent injury. This time is also used to reflect on what was learned during the session, set goals for the next class, or sometimes, just a quiet moment for the gymnasts to feel proud of their efforts and progress.

Navigating interactions with coaches and peers is another critical aspect of transitioning into professional gymnastics classes. Coaches are not just instructors; they are mentors who play a significant role in your child's gymnastics development. Respectful, clear communication is key.

The best coaches typically provide instructions and feedback in a direct yet supportive manner, focusing on what the gymnast can improve and how. Your child needs to learn to listen attentively, ask questions if they're unsure about a directive, and apply the feedback they receive. This interaction is a fundamental part of learning in a structured environment, as it teaches discipline and the importance of constructive criticism.

The way your child interacts with peers in the class also plays a significant role in their gymnastics experience. Gymnastics classes can foster a sense of team spirit and camaraderie among young athletes. Encourage your child to support their classmates, celebrate their successes, and offer encouragement during challenging moments. These interactions can help build a supportive network that makes learning more enjoyable and less intimidating.

The learning environment in a professional gymnastics class is designed to be both challenging and supportive. Giving constructive critiques is an essential component of this environment. Coaches provide regular assessments of each gymnast's progress, pointing out strengths and improvement areas.

This feedback is usually specific and actionable and is given in a way that aims to motivate, instruct, and not discourage. Understanding this can help you and your child realize that every correction or piece of advice is a stepping stone to becoming a better gymnast.

Finally, the adjustment period to professional gymnastics classes can vary from one child to another. It's normal for there to be a mix of excitement and nervousness. Setting realistic expectations can help manage any initial jitters.

Explain to your child that it's okay to feel a bit overwhelmed at first and that every gymnast in the room has been a beginner at some point. Encourage them to focus on their own progress rather than comparing themselves to others. Celebrate small victories and improvements as these are the markers of growth in this sport.

Remember, the goal of these first few classes is not just to learn gymnastics skills but to begin integrating into the structure and discipline of professional training, which is a valuable life skill in itself.

With each class, your child will gain physical strength and agility, confidence, resilience, and the joy of mastering new challenges. As you both adapt to this new phase, embrace the learning curve and look forward to the incredible leaps—both literal and figurative—yet to come.

8.4 Meeting with Coaches: Questions to Ask

When the time comes for your child to step into a more structured gymnastics program, meeting with potential coaches becomes a pivotal moment. It's not just about ensuring the coach has the right qualifications but also about understanding their approach to training young gymnasts and ensuring they prioritize safety and positive development. Here's how you can navigate this important interaction, ensuring you gather all the necessary information to make a well-informed decision.

Coach's Experience and Background

Understanding a coach's qualifications and experience is crucial, as this directly influences the quality of training your child will receive. Start by inquiring about their gymnastics background. Ask questions like, "How long have you been coaching young gymnasts?" and "What is your experience with gymnasts at my child's level?"

It's also helpful to ask about their formal training and certifications. Questions such as, "What certifications do you hold in gymnastics coaching?" or "Have you participated in any continuing education courses recently?" can provide insights into their commitment to professional growth. Discussing their journey and approach can give you a clearer picture of how they might inspire and push your child to achieve their best.

Safety Protocols

Your child's safety is paramount, and understanding the safety measures and protocols a coach follows should be at the forefront of your conversation. Inquire about their procedures for preventing injuries during training. Questions could include, "Can you walk me through your typical safety checklist for a training session?" or "How do you ensure the equipment is safe to use?"

Additionally, it's important to know how they handle injuries should they occur. Asking, "What steps do you take if a gymnast is injured during practice?" and "Can you provide examples of how you've handled past incidents?" helps assess their preparedness and responsiveness to potential accidents.

Communication and Feedback

Effective communication is key in any coaching relationship. It's important for coaches to clearly articulate instructions and provide constructive feedback. Ask the coach about their communication style with both gymnasts and parents.

Questions like, "How do you provide feedback to your gymnasts during and after practice?" and "How frequently do you communicate progress and areas for improvement to parents?" will help you understand how involved you can be in your child's development.

Additionally, it can be insightful to know how they handle situations where a gymnast might struggle with certain skills. Consider asking, "When a gymnast finds a skill challenging, how do you support them to overcome these challenges?"

Philosophy on Growth and Development

Finally, understanding a coach's philosophy on growth and development can significantly influence your decision. This goes beyond physical training to how they support young athletes' overall well-being and development. Inquire about their goals for gymnasts at different stages of their development.

Ask questions like, "What are your primary objectives for gymnasts in the beginning stages of training?" and "How do you balance pushing for performance with ensuring that gymnasts are not overwhelmed?"

Understanding their views on the importance of mental health is also beneficial. To that end, inquire how they support gymnasts in managing pressure and stress during competitions. This can provide a window into how they prepare athletes physically, mentally, and emotionally.

This dialogue with potential coaches is more than just an interview; it's an opportunity to build a partnership supporting your child's gymnastics growth.

Each answer will help paint a clearer picture of how the coach will influence your child's gymnastics journey, ensuring they are capable of teaching the skills necessary for the sport and committed to nurturing a positive, safe, and supportive environment for your child to thrive.

Remember, the right coach can make all the difference, turning training into a transformative experience that goes beyond the gym.

8.5 Preparing Mentally and Physically for Competitive Gymnastics

As your child advances in gymnastics, the intensity and demands of the sport also escalate. It's no longer just about having fun and learning new flips; it's about honing those skills to perfection and preparing for more serious competition.

The transition from recreational to competitive gymnastics is a significant step that requires diligent physical and mental preparation. Let's explore how you can support your child in strengthening their body and mind to meet these new challenges.

Physical Conditioning

Maintaining and enhancing physical fitness is crucial as your child moves into higher levels of competition. Gymnastics is a sport that demands a lot from the body—strength, flexibility, endurance, and explosive power. To help your child build these qualities, consider integrating various training activities into their routine.

Strength training is essential, but it should be age-appropriate. Lightweight resistance training, body-weight exercises like push-ups and pull-ups, and even some supervised weightlifting can be beneficial for building muscle strength and endurance.

Flexibility is another cornerstone of gymnastics, and daily stretching routines should be a non-negotiable part of training to improve range of motion and prevent injuries. Cardiovascular activities such as swimming, running, or cycling can enhance endurance, helping build stamina and overall fitness.

It's also wise to consult with a sports fitness coach who can tailor a conditioning program specific to your child's needs, focusing on areas that need improvement and ensuring that the training complements their gymnastics practices rather than over-whelming them.

Mental Preparation

The mental aspect of gymnastics is just as demanding as the physical, and this becomes even more important as their skill and pressure progress. Preparing your child mentally for the rigors of competitive gymnastics involves several strategies. We touched on these earlier but here's a quick refresher of a few:

- Goal setting is a powerful tool that helps focus effort and measure progress.
- Visualization; encourage your child to visualize themselves performing routines flawlessly. This mental rehearsal can enhance confidence and reduce anxiety before competitions.
- Coping with pressure is another critical skill. Teach your child relaxation techniques such as deep breathing or meditation to help manage stress during competitions.
- Discuss scenarios they might face during events and how they can handle them, which can prepare your child to deal with pressure effectively.

These mental preparation strategies can empower your child to perform their best, even under the stress of competition.

Understanding Competition

Familiarizing your child with the competitive landscape of gymnastics is important for setting realistic expectations and preparing them strategically for events. Educate them about the types and levels of competitions available, from local meets to national championships.

Talk through the structure of these competitions, the scoring system, and what judges typically look for in a routine. This knowledge can demystify competitions and reduce anxiety.

It's also helpful to attend a few competitions as spectators; this can be incredibly valuable, allowing your child to observe others, understand how events are run, and what to expect when they compete. Knowing the competitive environment prepares your child practically and helps build a competitive spirit and sportsmanship.

Balancing School and Gymnastics

As gymnastics training intensifies, so does the challenge of balancing it with academic responsibilities. This balancing act is essential for the well-being and development of your child.

Help your child learn to use a digital calendar or planner to schedule their schoolwork and gymnastics training. This helps in managing their time efficiently and ensures that neither academics nor gymnastics is neglected.

Teach them prioritization skills—understanding which tasks are most important and urgent can help them tackle their responsibilities effectively.

Also, open communication with teachers can be beneficial; they can provide support and may offer flexibility around major training events or competitions. Remember, the goal is to ensure that your child excels in both their academic and athletic pursuits without overwhelming themselves.

Preparing your child for competitive gymnastics involves a holistic approach, focusing on physical conditioning, mental readiness, understanding of the competitive landscape, and balancing life's other responsibilities.

As you guide your child through these preparations, your involvement and support are invaluable in helping them navigate the challenges and reap the rewards of competitive gymnastics.

8.6 The Role of Parents in Supporting Aspiring Gymnasts

Parents play a pivotal role that extends far beyond the role of a spectator cheering from the sidelines. Your involvement is crucial in providing the emotional and logistical support that helps young gymnasts thrive. Understanding how to effectively nurture and advocate for your child can make all the difference in their gymnastics experience, helping them grow not just as athletes but as confident and resilient individuals.

Emotional Support

The emotional landscape of gymnastics can be as challenging as the physical demands of the sport. Your child will likely face highs of triumph and lows of frustration or disappointment.

Your role in providing emotional support involves more than just consoling them after a tough practice or celebrating their successes. It's about helping them navigate their emotions and fostering a positive mindset.

Encourage them to express how they feel about their training and competitions, and listen actively to their concerns or fears. This open line of communication helps them process their experiences and reassures them that they're not alone in their journey.

Moreover, motivation from a parent can be a powerful catalyst. Focus on affirming their efforts rather than just their achievements. Phrases like "I'm proud of how hard you worked today" or "I noticed you really improved on your form" can boost their morale and motivate them to keep improving.

It's also important to help them set realistic expectations and manageable goals, which can prevent overwhelming feelings and help them stay committed and enthusiastic about their progress.

Logistical Support

The practical aspects of supporting a young gymnast involve a fair amount of organization and dedication from parents. From arranging transportation to practices and meets to managing their schedule to ensure they have enough time for school, rest, and gymnastics to handling the financial aspects of training, your support is indispensable.

Create a calendar that tracks their gymnastics events, academic deadlines, and other family activities. This helps them manage their time effectively and teaches them valuable lessons about prioritization and time management.

Financial considerations are also part of the logistical support. Gymnastics can be expensive, requiring you to pay for classes, club fees, uniforms, travel to competitions, and more. Planning in advance for these costs can alleviate financial stress.

Consider setting up a budget for gymnastics-related expenses and explore opportunities for scholarships or fundraising within your gymnastics community that can help manage the costs.

Advocacy for the Gymnast

As a parent, you are your child's advocate, especially in environments where they might not feel confident to speak up for themselves. It's important to ensure that your child's needs are met and they are treated fairly and respectfully in their gymnastics club.

This might mean speaking with coaches about any concerns regarding training practices or discussing your child's developmental needs. If your child is struggling with a particular aspect of their training, work with their coach to modify their routine or find additional resources to help them succeed.

Advocacy also involves being informed about the sport. Being in the know about gymnastics helps you connect with your child over their interest and enables you to make informed decisions regarding their training and development.

Take the time to learn about the sport, attend parent meetings, and engage with the gymnastics community. This knowledge helps navigate the gymnastics world and shows your child that you value and respect their passion.

Building a Home Support System

Creating a supportive home environment is crucial in reinforcing the values and lessons your child learns in gymnastics. This includes physical support, like ensuring they have a safe space at home to practice or stretch.

Emotional support is also key, providing encouragement and understanding, celebrating their efforts, and comforting them through disappointments. Additionally, involve other family members in their gymnastics journey. Whether it's attending competitions as a family or celebrating achievements together, this family involvement strengthens their support system and enriches their sporting experience.

In creating this nurturing environment, you help foster the qualities that gymnastics aims to develop in young athletes: discipline, resilience, and confidence. Your support helps them not just in their gymnastics pursuits but in all areas of their life, teaching them the importance of hard work, perseverance, and the value of a supportive community.

As this chapter closes, remember that your role as a parent is integral to your child's gymnastics experience. Your support helps them navigate the challenges and joys of the sport, building a foundation not only for athletic success but for lifelong resilience and confidence.

Conclusion

As we reach the final pages of our journey together in "Gymnastics for Kids: The Ultimate Beginner's Guide," I want to revisit our primary goal: to equip you and your child with a comprehensive, engaging, and most importantly, safe introduction to the world of gymnastics right from your home.

Whether you've transformed a small corner of your living room into a practice space or dedicated a whole room for gymnastics, the steps we've explored are designed to lay a solid foundation for your child's gymnastic adventures.

We started with the basics—setting up a safe practice environment, understanding key gymnastics terms, and introducing simple warm-up and stretching exercises. Each of these elements plays a critical role in ensuring that your child's gymnastics practice is both effective and safe.

We've covered essential gymnastics skills such as rolls, handstands, and cartwheels, and progressed to more challenging skills like handstand walking, round-offs, and basic flips. Remember, each skill builds on the last, helping your child grow stronger and more confident with each practice session.

Safety is paramount, as we've emphasized throughout this book. We've delved into the best practices for keeping young gymnasts safe, including using proper equipment, understanding the role of spotters, and maintaining a safe practice environment. These guidelines are crucial for preventing injuries and ensuring that gymnastics remains a joyful and healthy activity for your child.

The inspirational stories from the gymnastics world were included to motivate and teach valuable lessons about perseverance and success. These stories showcase the physical strength of famous gymnasts and their mental resilience and dedication to their craft.

Gymnastics is more than physical training; it's a mental and emotional journey. We've discussed setting realistic goals, overcoming fears, staying focused, managing frustrations, and the importance of celebrating every small victory along the way. These skills are essential for personal growth and will serve your child well beyond the gymnastics mat.

For those of you considering the transition from home practice to professional gymnastics classes, we've offered guidelines to help you evaluate readiness, choose the right gymnastics club, and prepare for the exciting world of competitive gymnastics. This transition is a significant step; being well-prepared will make it a smooth and positive experience for your child.

To all the parents reading this, your role in your child's gymnastics journey is invaluable. Your emotional support, logistical help, and advocacy create the environment in which your child can thrive. You are their cheerleader, coach, and teammate rolled into one.

As we conclude, I want to leave you with this powerful message: **Gymnastics offers a unique opportunity to build discipline, confidence, resilience, and joy in your child's life.** It's more than just a sport; it's a tool for growth and development.

I encourage you to take the first step, use the resources provided here, and enthusiastically embark on this gymnastic journey with your child. Share your experiences and progress with others. The community you build will be a source of encouragement and inspiration.

Here's to many successful flips, rolls, and jumps ahead!

Thank you for joining me on this exciting journey into the world of gymnastics! If this book has helped your child learn and have fun with gymnastics, I'd love for you to share your experience by leaving a review. Your feedback can help other young gymnasts discover the joy of flipping and tumbling, just like your child. It only takes a minute, but your review can inspire a whole new group of kids to get active and reach their dreams. Thank you for being part of this movement, and happy tumbling!

Visit this URL to leave a review: https://www.amazon.com/review/review-your-purchases/?asin=B0DDPZSYJ4

Or scan the QR code below:

References

1. Porch. (n.d.). How children can train for gymnastics at home. https://porch.com/advice/children-train-gymnastics-home

2. Practical Mama. (2016, June). DIY - How to build a balance beam. https://practicalmama.com/2016/06/diy-how-to-build-a-balance-beam/

3. Active Kids. (n.d.). The ultimate gymnastics glossary for clueless parents. https://www.activekids.com/gymnastics/articles/the-ultimate-gymnastics-glossary-for-clueless-parents

4. El Paso Times. (2016, September 24). "Nadia" balances story of young gymnast, country's hopes. https://www.elpasotimes.com/story/life/2016/09/24/nadia-balances-story-young-gymnast-countrys-hopes/90738452/

5. Gymnastics HQ. (n.d.). 9 basic gymnastics skills you should master. https://gymnasticshq.com/9-basic-gymnastics-skills-you-should-master/

6. Norbert's. (n.d.). Tips for maintaining and caring for gymnastics equipment. https://www.norberts.com/news/30/Tips-for-Maintaining-and-Caring-for-Gymnastics-Equipment.html

7. OrthoInfo. (n.d.). Gymnastics injury prevention - OrthoInfo - AAOS. https://orthoinfo.aaos.org/en/staying-healthy/gymnastics-injury-prevention

8. Technogym. (n.d.). The story of gymnast Katelyn Ohashi. https://www.technogym.com/us/newsroom/katelyn-ohashi-gymnast-motivation-champion/

9. Boston Children's Hospital. (n.d.). Sports injury prevention | Gymnastics. https://www.childrenshospital.org/sports-injury-prevention/gymnastics

10. Gymnastics HQ. (n.d.). Gymnastics skills: Event and level skill lists. https://gymnasticshq.com/gymnastics-skills/

11. SHIFT Movement Science. (n.d.). The ultimate guide to gymnastics strength. https://shiftmovementscience.com/ultimategymnasticsstrengthguide/

12. Tumbling Coach. (n.d.). 6 spotting techniques all tumbling coaches should know. https://tumblingcoach.com/blog/spotting-technique/

13. HiSawyer. (n.d.). 8 benefits of gymnastics for kids. https://www.hisawyer.com/blog/8-benefits-of-gymnastics-for-kids

14. Porch. (n.d.). How children can train for gymnastics at home. https://porch.com/advice/children-train-gymnastics-home

15. Gymnastics HQ. (n.d.). 10 beginner gymnastics skills you can practice at home. https://gymnasticshq.com/10-beginner-gymnastics-skills-you-can-practice-at-home/

16. Brightly. (n.d.). High-flying gymnastics books for kids and teens. https://www.readbrightly.com/gymnastics-books-for-kids-and-teens/

17. Positive Psychology. (n.d.). Boosting mental toughness in young athletes & 20 ... https://positivepsychology.com/mental-toughness-for-young-athletes/

18. Active Kids. (n.d.). Overcoming common sports fears in kids. https://www.activekids.com/sports/articles/overcoming-common-sports-fears-in-kids

19. Productive Recruit. (n.d.). The ultimate guide to SMART goals for student-athletes. https://productiverecruit.com/blog/smart-goals-for-student-athletes

20. The Mia Wave. (n.d.). The inspirational story of 12 year old gymnast Paige Calendine. https://themiawave.org/20073/features/the-inspirational-story-of-12-year-old-gymnast-paige-calendine/

21. OrthoInfo. (n.d.). Gymnastics injury prevention - OrthoInfo - AAOS. https://orthoinfo.aaos.org/en/staying-healthy/gymnastics-injury-prevention

22. NFHS. (n.d.). First aid, health and safety course. https://nfhslearn.com/courses/first-aid-health-and-safety

23. iTeh Standards. (2018). EN 913:2018 - Gymnastic equipment - General safety. https://standards.iteh.ai/catalog/standards/cen/1093ad79-3b50-4960-9129-416b15b27c1c/en-913-2018

24. Complete Performance Coaching. (2022, April 21). Spotting an athlete - and the myths surrounding it. https://completeperformancecoaching.com/2022/04/21/spotting-an-athlete-and-the-myths-surrounding-it/

25. Wikipedia. (n.d.). Dominique Moceanu. https://en.wikipedia.org/wiki/Dominique_Moceanu

26. Sanford Health. (n.d.). Gymnast learns lessons working back from serious knee injury. https://news.sanfordhealth.org/rehabilitation-therapy/gymnast-knee-injury-physical-therapy/

27. Superhero Jacked. (2020, April 18). Simone Biles workout and diet plan: Train like an Olympic. https://superherojacked.com/2020/04/18/simone-biles-workout/

28. KTVZ. (2024, February 18). Fisk University made history as the first HBCU gymnastics team, but the sport still struggles with diversity, gymnasts say. https://ktvz.com/news/national-world/cnn-

national/2024/02/18/fisk-university-made-history-as-the-first-hbcu-gymnastics-team-but-the-sport-still-struggles-with-diversity-gymnasts-say/

29. Lake City Twisters. (n.d.). Is your child ready for competitive gymnastics? - LCT. https://lakecitytwisters.com/is-your-child-ready-for-competitive-gymnastics/

30. Elite Gymnastics. (n.d.). Parents guide to choosing a gymnastics school. https://elitegymnast.com/parents-place/choosing-gymnastics-school/

31. Emeth Gym. (n.d.). First gymnastics classes: How to prepare (7 tips). https://emethgym.com/blog/first-gymnastics-classes-how-to-prepare-7-tips-emethgym/

32. Athleta Gymnastics. (n.d.). Tips for parents to support young gymnasts. https://www.athletagymnastics.com.au/page-blog.html?p=tips-parents-support-young-gymnasts

Made in the USA
Monee, IL
21 October 2025